NO BONES ABOUT IT

INCREASE YOUR BONE DENSITY
WITHOUT MEDICATION

Jayne M. Wesler

Cover design by Rob Williams ilovemycover.com

First Printing: March 2021

Milford, PA

Saint Cloud, FL

ISBN 978-1-7355405-2-8

Library of Congress Control Number: 2021904090

Published by Phoenix Consultation & Advocacy LLC

Jayne M. Wesler, Esq., LCSW

JayneWesler.com

WeslerBooks.com

WHY READ THIS BOOK?

Ms. Wesler has a bone to pick with the medical community and the dairy industry. Since you picked up this book, it is likely that this topic cuts you close to the bone as well. Have you been diagnosed with osteopenia or osteoporosis? Has your doctor recommended medication to increase your bone density? Did your doctor tell you that those medications can increase your risk of esophageal cancer, osteosarcoma, osteonecrosis of the jaw, atypical femoral fracture, cardiovascular death, heart attack, and stroke?

Since she was a young woman of 25, Jayne Wesler recognized that she was at risk for contracting osteoporosis when she got older. How did she know? She had several risk factors: she was female; she had a small bone structure; she was Caucasian; and she was a lightweight.

For those reasons, she took precautions throughout her adult life. She was a tea drinker, so she added milk to counteract any negative effect of the caffeine. And not just any milk, but concentrated dry milk. It made the tea creamier and more satisfying, and gave her lots of extra calcium.

In addition, she did frequent weight-bearing exercise. She ran. She lifted weights. She was at the gym twelve hours a week, rotating the focus on different body parts: legs on day one, chest and biceps on day two, and triceps, back, and shoulders on day three. Abs were every day.

She had always eaten well. Lots of fresh fruits and vegetables. Poultry and fish. Low fat dairy. Whole grains.

When Ms. Wesler turned 50, her doctor put her on calcium and vitamin D. After four years of taking those supplements, she expected her DEXA scan to show positive results. Yet her doctor visit on June 1, 2015 was equivalent to a terror attack. On her. With no one to call for help.

She was 54 years old.

Thus began a year-long journey to find out:

Why her bones were "thinning at an alarming rate," according to her primary doctor;

Why he intended to let this continue for another 18 months with no additional intervention;

What was causing her alarming bone loss; and ?

What she could do about it.

Ms. Wesler would like to help you get answers to your bone issues, and to learn how to increase your bone density without medication.

Open this book to find out more! Learn how Ms. Wesler figured out how to increase her own bone density. If she can do it, you can, too!

Jayne Wesler is available to speak at your event, group, or workforce on a variety of topics, including increasing bone density without medication, emotional tears, the biology of men and women which affects why women cry more often than men, why men and women are equally hormonal, and to teach EFT. Contact her at her website JayneWesler.com.

OTHER BOOKS BY JAYNE WESLER

The HANDBOOK FOR PARENTS OF CHILDREN WITH SPECIAL NEEDS: A THERAPEUTIC AND LEGAL APPROACH

As a lawyer, psychotherapist, and former Child Study Team member who practiced exclusively on behalf of children with special needs, Jayne Wesler has helped hundreds, if not thousands, of parents obtain educational programs which led to their child's success. In this book, she shares information with you from federal and state law, federal and state regulations, psychotherapeutic techniques, and her experience so that you, too, can change the trajectory of your child's life. If you use the techniques, tools, and knowledge she provides to you, you can and will obtain successful programs for your child to help them succeed in school—the sooner, the better.

Children grow so quickly that, when they do need help, they need it now. Don't wait. Do it today. You'll be glad you did.

"This book is an easy to read go-to manual

containing pearls of wisdom and accessible references for creating your child's educational blueprint. Jayne Wesler created this handbook blending both wisdom and heart!"

Jill Brooks, Ph.D, Clinical Neuropsychologist, Head 2 Head Consulting

"With her background as a psychotherapist and an education attorney, Jayne Wesler has written a thoughtful and practical guide for parents of children with special needs looking to navigate the sometimes turbulent and confusing waters of the special education world."

Daniel DaSilva, Ph.D., Pediatric Neuropsychologist, Morris Psychological Group

"This is an essential guide for parents seeking the best education for their children, important information from an expert attorney, educator, and psychotherapist. A must read."

Ellen Fenster-Kuehl, Ph.D., Licensed Psychologist

"The book you hold in your hand is a blueprint to navigating the complexities of educational programming. Attorney and psychotherapist Jayne Wesler integrates her knowledge and offers a unique perspective on how to truly transform your child's life."

Melissa Fiorito-Grafman, Ph.D, Clinical Neuropsychologist, Center for Neuropsychology & Psychotherapy

"Attorney and psychotherapist Jayne Wesler shares her practical knowledge on how to truly transform your child's life."

Dana Henning, Ed.D., Education Consultant, Dana Henning Training Programs.

HURTS SO GOOD
AN ORGASM OF TEARS

Have you ever had a good cry? Maybe it is rare for you, or maybe it happens at the drop of a hat.

Have you ever wondered about the biology of tears?

Have you ever noticed the physical aspects of your emotional tears? Quivering abs? The prick of tears in your eyes? Chest tightening? Throat hurting? Nostrils flaring? Mouth crumpling?

Have you ever been scolded or criticized for crying?

Would it intrigue you to know that there are significant similarities between emotional tears and orgasm?

Join me to delve into this most baffling of human behaviors: the shedding of emotional tears or, as we know it in the vernacular, a 'good cry.'

Jayne Wesler has played many roles in her life. From the newsroom to the intense hush of psychotherapy sessions in various venues, including a locked psychiatric unit in a large urban hospital, to trying cases in courtrooms in Newark, Trenton, and Atlantic City, New Jersey, Ms. Wesler has been both witness to, and actor in, the most intense of human dramas. Trained by experts at GCU and NYU to use her emotions as a tool, Ms. Wesler is able to tap into human experience to help educate and heal others. In this riveting expose, Ms. Wesler illuminates the parallels between orgasm and emotional tears, thereby demonstrating a biological legitimacy to the need for a good cry. Just as sex is the all-time, one-and-only treatment for epididymal hypertension, commonly known as "Blue Balls," a good cry is the only remedy for a frustrated and achy soul—a Blue Heart.

HURTS SO GOOD:
AN ORGASM OF TEARS
WORKBOOK

Learn how to deepen your most important relationships with exercises for emotional intimacy. You will be surprised how much your trust and your love for yourself and your partner will deepen when you utilize the activities and exercises in this extraordinary book.

My tears are my gift to you.
They mean I trust you; I am making myself vulnerable to you; I am opening myself up to you; I am taking the risk of being hurt to deepen my bonds with you.
Maybe even I love you.

Jayne M. Wesler is an author, coach, speaker, licensed clinical social worker, and attorney. She is the author of Handbook for Parents of Children with Special Needs: A Therapeutic and Legal Approach; Hurts So Good: An Orgasm of Tears; Hurts So Good: An Orgasm of Tears Workbook; and No Bones About It: Increase Your Bone Density Without Medication. Ms. Wesler is a partner in the law firm of Sussan, Greenwald and Wesler, and for decades has helped students with disabilities obtain the kind of educational programming that helps them achieve success. As a university student, Ms. Wesler worked as a journalist and has always been a writer at heart.

While in training to become a psychotherapist, a mentor told Ms. Wesler that she carried "a lot of emotion." This has proven to be both an advantage and a disadvantage, but in her training, Ms. Wesler has used her own emotions as a powerful tool to help others.

For many years, Ms. Wesler has seen society equate women and femininity with weakness. This has been particularly galling for her as she comes from a long line of strong women, has withstood many significant challenges in her own life, and has successfully overcome them. She knows in a very personal way the strength that underlies emotional tears.

As a psychotherapist, Ms. Wesler has worked with adults, teens, and children in various settings, including both inpatient and outpatient, individual and group therapy. As a member of multiple Child Study Teams, Ms. Wesler conducted evaluations, wrote IEP's, case-managed elementary students, high-school students, and students placed in specialized private school programs. She also developed and facilitated various psychotherapy groups .

Early in her legal career, Ms. Wesler practiced at a large New Jersey law firm where she founded the Special Education Law Section. Earlier, she served as a judicial clerk to the Hon. Clarkson S. Fisher Jr., then presiding judge of the Chancery Division for the Superior Court of Monmouth County, New Jersey.

Ms. Wesler also served as a law clerk for the

Monmouth County, New Jersey, Prosecutor's Office, Appellate Division, where she did a special research project for the Monmouth County Prosecutor regarding the prosecution of cases involving repressed memory of sexual abuse. As a licensed clinical social worker and an attorney, Ms. Wesler is experienced in the fields of special education, mental health, and psychotherapy.

Ms. Wesler has presented continuing education workshops on various topics in the fields of law and mental health, including IDEIA, Section 504 plans, and the discipline of students with disabilities. She has written a scholarly paper on the Americans with Disabilities Act of 1990 and a study in conjunction with the Hon. Thomas N. Lyon, Judge of the Superior Court of New Jersey, Union County, concerning the proper treatment of cases involving litigants with mental illness.

Ms. Wesler earned her Juris Doctor degree from Seton Hall University School of Law; her M.S.W. degree from New York University School of Social Work in New York City; and her B.S.W. degree, *summa cum laude*, from Georgian Court University. She is admitted to practice in New Jersey, the United States District Court for the District of New Jersey, and the Third Circuit Court of Appeals.

In her spare time, Ms. Wesler enjoys spending time with family and friends, hiking, skiing, scuba diving, snorkeling, working out, reading, traveling, and cooking.

Come, my friends,

Tis not too late to seek a newer world.

Push off, and sitting well in order smite

The sounding furrows; for my purpose holds

To sail beyond the sunset, and the baths

Of all the western stars, until I die.

It may be that the gulfs will wash us down:

It may be we shall touch the Happy Isles,

And see the great Achilles, whom we know.

Though much is taken, much abides; and though

We are not now that strength which in old days

Moved earth and heaven, that which we are, we are;

One equal temper of heroic hearts,

Made weak by time and fate, but strong in will

To strive, to seek, to find, and not to yield.

From *Ulysses* by Alfred Tennyson (1809-1892)

TABLE OF CONTENTS

CHAPTER ONE
BROKEN: THE DIAGNOSIS

The purpose of this book is to reach the millions of women and men who are diagnosed with bone loss and to give them, and maybe you, dear Reader, a viable alternative to taking medication to increase their bone density.

Have you gotten a diagnosis of osteopenia or osteoporosis? Has someone you love been diagnosed? If you are freaking out and wondering what you can do, take a deep breath. **There are steps you can take to strengthen your bones**. This diagnosis does not define your life now or in the future. Keep reading to learn how you can assess your risk factors, summon and utilize your resources, and make positive changes in the health of your bones.

Ernest Hemingway said, **"The world breaks everyone and afterward many are strong at the broken places."**

This is a noble and inspiring quote, and it is helpful to

buoy up our spirits in times of difficult challenges. However, how many of us want to volunteer to be broken further than life has broken us already?

The emotional impact of getting a diagnosis of osteopenia or osteoporosis can be staggering. After all, once you lose your skeleton, that's it. Game over. You cannot get a skeletal transplant.

I know this in a very personal way as I was diagnosed with osteoporosis at a very early age. Unexpectedly, I might add. I was doing everything right. I ate well. I had exercised a lot for years, including significant amounts of weight-bearing exercise. At 55 years old, I was fairly young to get such a diagnosis. Yet, there I was, in my doctor's office, hearing the words that no one wants to hear: "Your bones are thinning at an alarming rate."

My litigation attorney brain went into recovery and cross-examination mode. I had a limited amount of time with my doctor, and I needed to find out what exactly had happened, why it had happened, and, most important, what I could do about it.

My doctor was well-thought of; he had a great reputation, and he had earned it. He took time to talk with me, but the conversation did not go anywhere satisfactory. He gave me the standard narrative of all the things I could do to increase my bone density. Eat more dairy products. Take calcium supplements. Walk.

Well, duh. I had been doing that and so much more for decades. I explained that to him, and asked him what was causing my bone loss. He did not know. I asked him what else I could do to prevent further "alarming" bone loss. He could not answer that question.

At this point, I began to feel quite frustrated, and pressed him further. Finally, exasperated, he burst out with, "Eat more ice cream!" and then he chuckled. Perhaps he was frustrated, too. I knew him to be an excellent physician. I knew he really cared about me. He cared about all of his patients, and he invested his time and his skill to ensure he kept us in the best of health. But when he told me to eat more ice cream, and then he laughed, it felt like a door slamming shut. As in, I am not getting any more out of this avenue. There is no more wisdom here for me, no more knowledge. I felt as if I had stepped out into a vast emptiness that I had to navigate for myself.

Navigate I did. For about a year, I sought and found answers. Some things worked, and some things gave me a lot of other types of trouble. At the end of that first year, though, I discovered something uplifting, positive, and sweetly relieving: I had increased my own bone density, without medication. It was the result of my own determination, persistence, and perseverance. I believed I could do it, and I did.

There was no magic answer. I tried many different interventions, including dietary changes, the addition of complementary supplements, and additional types and amounts of exercise. I was willing to try whatever it took to strengthen my skeleton. For me, it was as dramatic as life or death. I was very young to have such bone loss, despite all of my lifelong healthy habits. I did not want to suffer a fractured hip at a young age, develop pneumonia, and die. I also did not want to take prescription medications that had side effects which ranged from physical discomfort to lethal disease. Determined, I persisted to look for answers.

Bodies age. Bones do often thin as we grow older. While I believe in growing old gracefully, and in gracefully surrendering the things of youth, I also believe we can work at staying strong and vibrant as we age. What I am saying is, we cannot prevent aging, but we can influence its outcome. If you want to stay strong and keep your bones strong, too, you will have to work at it. But there is joy in that work. There is a deep physical, mental, and emotional satisfaction in working your body so that it stays healthy.

If you have been diagnosed with bone loss and are interested in trying more conservative, and possibly healthier and less harmful, interventions to increase your bone density, I urge you to continue reading this book. If you do, if you are honest with yourself about your lifestyle and your habits, and if you are willing to employ the interventions I have set forth in this book, it is likely that you can increase your bone density without taking prescription medication.

The specific purposes of this book are:

- To offer hope to people diagnosed with osteopenia and osteoporosis.
- To offer non-medication interventions to those diagnosed with osteopenia and osteoporosis.
- To raise awareness that interventions other than medicine exist to increase bone density.
- To generate interest in treating osteopenia and osteoporosis without medication.
- To generate a network of interested consumers.
- To develop public interest in these interventions.
- To facilitate the sharing of information and knowledge.
- To encourage people to engage in medical self-advocacy.
- To help men and women be and stay healthier as they age.
- Ultimately to have non-medication interventions be the first treatment choice for osteopenia and osteoporosis.

Bone loss occurs naturally as we age. However, if you: learn what your predisposing factors to bone loss are, take steps to minimize those factors, learn and utilize interventions which are proven to strengthen bones, then it is likely that you, too, can increase your bone density without medication.

It's worth a try, isn't it? Come, turn the pages and hear my story. Focus on the evidence. Do not start taking medication out of panic. Make sure you understand your options. Wait until then to decide which path is right for you.

CHAPTER TWO
JAYNE'S STORY

My gynecologist, Dr. Alan Rote,[1] was bug-eyed as he burst through the door of the office where I sat. It was March of 2011, and I had never seen him in such a state, although I had known him for more than twenty-seven years.

"I've got your test results," he stated without preamble. "The numbers aren't good." He proceeded to read me the results of my very first DEXA scan. Although I was only just fifty years old, my bones appeared about twenty years older.

Dr. Rote proceeded to talk to me as if he were reading from a script. He described all the things I should do to keep my bones strong: I had to start taking calcium supplements, he said. I had to do weight-bearing exercise, he said. Walking was great, he said.

As if I did not know this already! Since I was in my early twenties, I have been aware that I was at risk for

---

[1]All names of physicians have been changed to protect their privacy.

developing osteoporosis later in life. I had many of the predisposing factors: I was female, Caucasian, with small bones, and weighed less than 127 pounds. For those reasons, I had always been careful to consume enough calcium and to do everything I could to keep my bones strong. I did not drink coffee. When I drank tea, I put dry milk in it to offset any potential negative effect of the caffeine, which (it was thought) can leach calcium from your bones. I did not drink soda or any carbonated beverages; these can eat away your bones as well.[2] I consumed plenty of dairy products like high-quality Greek yogurt, cottage cheese, and near-copious amounts of dry milk in my tea. I was a gym rat, running and weight-lifting most days. What did I need walking for?

This information really knocked me for a loop. Dr. Rote's script-like delivery of potential interventions I should undertake only added to the surreal nature of the moment. Where was the warm friend whom I had come to know and love over the decades since he had delivered my second child?

I left Dr. Rote's office shell-shocked. I needed some time to take it all in. Given my lifestyle, my Mediterranean diet, and my relentless exercise, my bones should have been in great shape. Yet the evidence to the contrary was

---

[2] Studies have demonstrated that cola beverages leach calcium, but that other carbonated beverages may not be harmful.

staring me in the face.

It took a little while, but I made peace with this information and made some changes. Chief among them was the addition of calcium supplements to my diet. I continued to do as much exercise as I could. Unfortunately, an old back injury had started to rear its irritating head: every time I picked up a dumbbell, my lower back would hurt, spasm, and threaten to go "out." That had happened a few times, and it had immobilized me.

When I was thirty-two years old, I started weightlifting with a partner for the first time ever. Naturally independent and ambitious, I had found I could cover more ground in anything I did if I were alone. At that time, I had become interested in serious bodybuilding, and accepted the offer of a young man to be his weightlifting partner. We worked easily together and, with him as a spotter, I was able to challenge myself, lift heavier weight, and add more muscle.

One day at the gym, I sat at a ninety-degree angle on the power leg press, my legs up in the air with my feet on the pedals. I had about eighty percent of my bodyweight on the rack. I started my first set. Down came the weight, until my knees were almost completely bent. That is when I heard, and felt, a distinct POP! in my lower left back. My partner had to help lift the weight up until I could roll out from underneath. I could not stand up straight, and foolishly continued to lift weights while bent over at nearly a right angle.

Long story short, I went to the chiropractor, who adjusted my back and made it functional. Since that time, however, it has remained a weak spot. As I got a little older, some things would trigger it occasionally, rendering me unable to walk or support my own weight. As I neared the half-century mark, the trigger turned out to be any time I lifted a pair of dumbbells.

For a period of time, I had to stop weightlifting altogether. When the pain in my back grew unbearably tedious—which is saying a lot, since I come from a stoic family who bears pain as their natural lot in life—I went to see my general practitioner, or GP, an internist called Dr. Mykos.

Dr. Mykos heard the whole story and told me two things I never forgot.

"Go to yoga," he said. "It will take away your back pain. And start having regular massage with a massage therapist."

I received those two directives as if he had written them on a prescription pad. I immediately found a local yoga studio and signed up. It turned out to be great timing, since it was December and everyone appeared to be too busy Christmas shopping and making holiday cookies to go to yoga. That's what happens, right? The first thing we drop is self-care. It was a boon for me, however, as I had the yoga instructor to myself for the first two weeks. I got very lucky meeting Carmel Calgano of Yoga Anjuli in Belmar, New Jersey. She taught me things that I have never forgotten. In the intervening years, I have taken classes with a number of other instructors, but Carmel remains a shining light in her field. I got a referral for a massage therapist and at first went weekly until my back was in better shape. Both of these interventions proved to be very effective at keeping my disabling back pain at bay. I credit yoga in particular for fixing my back. If I maintain my yoga practice, my back is as good as cured.

Despite the strength and flexibility I had gained in my back, it took me years to be able to lift weights regularly. Meanwhile, it was time for my next DEXA scan. After the first startling DEXA scan, Dr. Rote had encouraged me to have my GP monitor my bone density. Although this was good medical practice, I think Dr. Rote himself was traumatized by my poor bone density and preferred to have the GP deal with it.

My new DEXA scan results were disheartening. My bones had continued their downhill trend and had continued to lose significant density, despite the addition of calcium supplements to my already-enviable diet and exercise regimen. Dr. Mykos added vitamin D to my daily supplements. I did not, and still do not understand, why this was not prescribed two years earlier, but, okay, this was a new intervention and maybe it would do the trick.

Meanwhile life continued to be very busy. As a litigation attorney at a boutique "war" practice, I fielded calls for help at all hours of the day and night, and worked very long days, leaving as early as 4:45 am and returning home as late as 11:30 pm. Needless to say, sleep was a luxury, as was calm and quiet. Every day was a heart-pounding demand. My clients were twice-vulnerable children with special needs, so that raised the stakes—and the worry. Caught in the grip of this flowing river of life, the next two years passed swiftly. Before I knew it, it was time for my next DEXA scan.

For some reason, I had no trepidation in advance of my visit with the doctor to get the results. Perhaps it was because I was so busy and had been so health-conscious and so healthy that I did not think anything bad would happen to me physically or medically. Ignorance was bliss, at least until June 1, 2015.

That was the day Dr. Mykos sat across from me in one of his examination rooms and said,

"Your bones are thinning at an alarming rate."

What? Did I hear that correctly? This was not what I had been expecting. In fact, I had no specific expectations except that things would be fine. Except they weren't. Not by a long shot.

Yet here I was, only 54 years old, and Dr. Mykos was telling me I had the skeleton of a much-older woman. He gave it to me straight: I had a 10 % b‹ loss in the femoral neck of both my right and left h . when compared to the previous scan taken two years earlier. Since I had already suffered post-menopausal bone loss, this was not good news. The cumulative loss was severe: a T value of negative three point four (-3.4) in the left femoral neck and a negative two point seven (-2.7) in the right femoral neck. Both numbers were greater than the measure for osteoporosis, which is anything less than negative two point five (-2.5) .

Needless to say, this was terrifying. What made it worse was that Dr. Mykos could not explain *why* this was happening to me. I do recall he said it was a good thing I had never smoked, as that would have wreaked further havoc on my already-alarmingly-thin bones.

As I sat with him in the examining room, I strived to collect my thoughts and to use my time with the doctor wisely. It was difficult as I fought down a whirlwind of panicked thoughts. But when your doctor tells you, for the second time, that your DEXA scan results are "scary," panic does set it.

And panic I did.

To his credit, Dr. Mykos did talk about Forteo, a drug that builds bones and retards the breakdown of bone. He told me I was in danger of breaking my hip, and that I had a frail bone structure.

Frail. I, who have always gotten compliments on my

physical appearance and fitness. I, who people routinely mistook as younger because of my fitness level. I, whose strength, when assessed before beginning a regimen with a personal trainer, was off the charts when compared to women 25 and 30 years younger than I.

Yes. Me.

Dr. Mykos also told me I could no longer ski. Strike two at my heart. He also advised me not to ride horses. Strike three.

This really broke my heart, for I had just returned to this activity after a 40-year hiatus. Forty years of tragedy, loss, and striving for a better life. After four decades of gut-wrenching, self-sacrificing hard work, I was discovering a better life, giving to myself after a 40-year drought. It had felt wonderful and had also stung a little, like healing tears.

The horseback riding would have also brought me closer to my daughter, an equestrian in her heart of hearts and an accomplished horsewoman. I had pictured idyllic days at the barn, tending to the farm and the horses and riding them, too.

Now that dream came crashing to the earth, but I hardly noticed. I was too busy trying not to drown in my panic, to listen to what the doctor was saying, and to ask all the right questions.

He was telling me that I was too young for these numbers, the numbers that showed my bones were as thin as someone twenty or thirty years older. He told me he would keep me on 1800 mg of calcium daily and increase my dose of vitamin D to 4000 mg per day, 2000 in the morning and 2000 in the evening.

But this was really nothing new, I wanted to shout at him, nothing radical enough to address this medical emergency. After all, I had been taking 2000 mg of calcium per day for two years. At that time, when I was 52 years old, my DEXA scan showed a T-score of -2.8 in the left femoral neck and -2.4 in the right femoral neck. It was the area known as Ward's triangle, Dr. Mykos explained to me, where most fractures occur.

"It's a little distressing," he said back then of my results, my "numbers." He talked about the possibility of drug therapy. He told me about Evista, which solidifies and strengthens bones. That would be the first drug he would recommend. If that did not work, he would suggest Forteo, an injectable drug. If that did not work, he would prescribe a third drug called Prolia. But Prolia scared him, he said. The way it suppressed the body's osteoclast cells—the cells that break down bone—made him feel as if he were playing God when he prescribed it.

At that time, when I was 52 years old, Dr. Mykos did not recommend I take any medication. He said we would "hold off" because of my age. "Two years from now, things may get a lot worse," he said, and he did not believe I would fracture in the next two years. He recommended I take the calcium and we would do a repeat DEXA scan in two years.

Fast forward two years. By 2015, when I was 54, things *had* gotten a lot worse, but he was not giving me any other options or interventions. He planned to simply keep me on the same dose of calcium and Vitamin D. I wanted to know what *else* we were going to do to stop this perilous forward momentum. After all, once the skeleton disappears, you cannot simply order a new one on Amazon. In addition, to my knowledge, no one has ever done a skeleton transplant to date. And I did not want to be the first. As if it were even possible.

Drawing on my courtroom experience and ability to think on my feet, I had a list of questions and information I believed I needed. I asked him what else I could do. He said he was shocked at these numbers.

"You're too young for these numbers," he said to me.

Idea "Ok," I asked again, "what can I do?" He said I should get fifteen minutes of sun per day. He said I could eat sardines. He said I could walk with weights.

While these suggestions might all be somewhat helpful, their intervention did not seem likely to counteract the rapid disappearance of my skeleton. With all due respect, I had already been doing many interventions, and nothing was working. I pressed him further for answers.

"Okay," he said, "eat more ice cream." And chuckled.

That is really what I remember. That one-liner in response to my anguish. And the laugh. He really did look amused. I was not. Amused, that is. How could I be? It wasn't funny. I was desperate.

I also realized that he didn't get it. I was eating dairy, all the time. Plain low-fat Greek yogurt. The good stuff. No added sugar. No added anything. First Fage, then I discovered Siggi's. Low-fat cottage cheese. Low-fat milk. I exercised, I lifted weights, I did yoga. What was going on? Why were my bones disappearing faster than the beat of a hummingbird's wings?

I left Dr. Mykos's office that afternoon in what I now know was a fight-or-flight mindset. Total panic. All I could think about was, *What can I do?* I felt very much alone. I believed I had to find my own answers.

When I arrived home that evening after my fateful appointment, I started reviewing all the research I could find. Little did I know then the long and winding road I would follow.

The Journey Begins

My experience that day has led me to many insights

and discoveries. Would I trade those discoveries for a good solid skeleton? I do not know, but I am glad I did not have the choice, because maybe I would have chosen the easy way out and missed everything I learned in the next two years.

The most important lesson may have been to listen to my own voice and to trust myself. I know that everyone says this. There is a reason we hear, see, and read this sage advice over and over and over again. Please allow me to illustrate with a personal example.

After I left Dr. Mykos's office that Monday afternoon, I went straight home and started reviewing the literature on how to increase bone density. The first thing I came across was a study by a man in Florida which proved that dried plums—formerly known as prunes—increased bone density. Another study showed red grapefruit would do it. Yet another study said that any caffeine would have a negative impact on bones. I quit drinking tea. I ate 15 prunes every day, mimicking the study. I ate grapefruit. I started drinking forty-eight ounces of green tea every day after seeing another study on its efficacious effect on the skeleton. I read more studies. I bought a couple of books on the subject that looked promising. One was by an American assistant professor of nutrition and wellness who advanced a theory that we must maintain the alkalinity of our bloodstream or our bodies would increase that level by leaching the calcium from—you guessed it—our bones. The author had done a meta-review of thousands of research studies from all over the world on exactly who gets osteoporosis and who does not. The results were surprising and convincing.

The evidence presented in the book appeared unassailable. As a lawyer, hard data and evidence are important to me. In my desperate state, I grabbed onto her theory like a life jacket. Over a period of about three weeks, I changed over to a mostly vegan diet, drank no caffeine whatsoever (except for the green tea), and walked like a drum majorette on speed.

Although I had always been a gym rat and had done extensive cardio exercise, I had avoided high-impact running for years—since pre-menopause—due to its effect on my back and feet. For cardio exercise, I rode an elliptical machine instead. That was a great loss for me, since the strength and freedom I had felt while running had always made my heart sing. I recall sharing with my university classmates how I had been out running in the rain. When they all looked at me cross-eyed and asked why, I burst out with, "Because that's what life and living is all about!!" That was how much freedom and joy it gave me.

One thing that became obvious to me after June 1, 2015, was that elliptical training was not preventing my bone loss because it lacks the necessary impact on the heel and up the spine. Unfortunately, even after my doctors discovered I had osteopenia and osteoporosis at the age of 50, they did not share this news with me. Perhaps they did not know. But I learned it from my own experience, and started walking instead.

And walk I did. Like a mad woman. Walking, walking, walking. Fast. And far. Every day for an hour. Which is hard to do when your life is already overtaxed by a demanding career and a long commute. Meanwhile, I continued to eat prunes and grapefruit, drink green tea, and eat a low-acid diet. And pray.

A low-acid diet is not what it sounds like. At first blush, you might guess that you cannot eat anything containing acid, like citrus fruits or soda, right?

Wrong. Think again! Of course, no one should be drinking soda. Soda is unhealthy. Period. Diet soda is even worse than regular soda. But all soda is harmful, putting the consumer at higher risk of obesity, diabetes, heart disease, kidney malfunction, reproductive problems (due to BPA lining of soda cans), cancer, dehydration, vascular problems, and dental caries. The list of doom goes on and on, but you get the point. Don't drink it! Contrary to first blush, however, foods that contain acid do not necessarily make the blood (and urine—which you can test; I did) acidic. In fact, it is the animal foods that create the highest levels of acid in the bloodstream.[3] So in order to keep the blood alkaline, you should eat more fruits and vegetables and less — animal foods.[4] The author of the meta-analysis book, Amy Joy Lanou, Ph.D., includes a list of common foods with assigned positive and negative values so the reader can figure out how to keep the diet alkaline-producing. Unfortunately, the list is limited. Through my review of sources, I did find a much more comprehensive list at a gout website.

I sought an expert to help me figure out what was causing the osteoporosis so I could combat it at its source. At that point, I would have flown anywhere in the country, possibly even in the world, to get knowledgeable help, but I could find no such person. On the National Osteoporosis Foundation website, I found the name of a physician who was touted to be a bone density specialist, Dr. DeFelice. I made an appointment for July 30, 2015. While I waited to see her, I continued to read and to take stock of what I was doing.

First, I asked myself, "What is causing my osteoporosis?"

Second, I listed all the potential causes:

1.   Sedentary job

---

[3] Lanou, Amy Joy et al. *Building Bone Vitality*. McGraw Hill 2009.
[4] Ibid.

2. Less weightlifting due to back issues

3. High acid diet

4. Lack of calcium absorption

5. Lower impact cardio—elliptical

6. Other: hyperparathyroidism. Did my doctor test for this? My mom had suffered a parathyroid malfunction. This can throw off one's calcium level, and can be a low-incidence cause of osteoporosis. Had my doctor tested for diabetes, thyrotoxicosis, Cushing syndrome, or rheumatoid arthritis?

7. The black, caffeinated tea which I love and have drunk often for years.

Turns out, none of these was the culprit. But I did not know that then.

Third, I made a plan of corresponding interventions to combat each of the suspected sources:

1. Order a stand-and-walk desk for my office, where I sat for approximately twelve or more hours per day.

2. Schedule weight training with lower weight that would not cause back problems.

3. Switch diet to less meat and dairy and more plant-based. Eat veggies and dried fruit to reduce acid load per meal when eating higher-acid foods. Eat daily grapefruit, prunes, and drink green tea.

4. I was not sure how to combat the lack of

calcium absorption, if it were occurring.

5. Daily walking. Could I return to running, I wondered? Should I run? It might cause the bursitis in my feet to recur, trading one problem for another.

6. Get tested for hyperparathyroidism and any other medical conditions that could be causing my bones to thin.

7. Decrease my consumption of caffeinated tea.

Other interventions and considerations I listed included:

- Prayer
- See a nutritionist
- Acupuncture
- Try something new: CrossFit? Top sports physical therapist?
- Other minerals? Boron? Vitamin K?
- Decrease sugar (Although I did not use it or consume it in prepared goods or add it to my food or beverages, I did like honey in my tea at times).
- Be mindful of Z scores and fracture risk. Most physicians seem to concern themselves with T scores, but Z scores are important. T-scores are "the comparison of your results with young adults of the same sex at the time of peak bone mass,"

writes Diane L. Schneider, MD.[5] Conversely, Z-scores are "the comparison with individuals of the same age and ethnicity from a reference database. For example, if you are female, age fifty-five, and Asian, your Bone Mineral Density, or BMD, results for each region are compared to a reference group of fifty-five-year-old Asian women."[6] My Z scores were -2.4 in the left hip and -1.7 in the right hip. Not great, but much better and more encouraging than my T scores.

- Look at my Bone Mineral Content—BMC—if possible. It seemed that this three-dimensional measure would give a more accurate picture of the bone's strength. Find out how to test it.

- Osteoporosis is over-diagnosed in persons of petite stature because the reference populations are calculated from the values of large people.

- Technical accuracy and precision of BMD measurements are considered by some to be barely satisfactory for clinical use. An accurate measurement would represent the true mineral content of the targeted bone site. But DEXA error can occur in various ways: degenerative changes, scoliosis, the presence of foreign bodies, erroneous data entry,

---

[5] Schneider, Diane L. MD. *The Complete Book of Bone Health.* Prometheus Books. New York. 2011, p 72.
[6] Ibid.

incorrect measurement settings, failure to calibrate, improper calibration, and errors in computer programming. Individual errors can yield false results between 1% and 37%. [7] When we are monitoring our bone density, big differences in accuracy or uniformity between machines may make the results unreliable.

- Low bone mineral density does not explain fragility or fracture risk or rate.
- NORA (National Osteoporosis Risk Assessment) says that 82% of fractures occurred in people with high, medium or low bone density (osteopenia) and not those with osteoporosis.
- Referral to expert for bone formation, bone health, and nutrition.
- Hip fracture rates are falling despite alleged increase in osteoporosis.

My appointment with Dr. DeFelice arrived and I went eagerly. I really needed some expert help; I still felt all alone and did not know what to do to solve the riddle of my rapid bone loss.

To prepare for the appointment, I had a succinct and pertinent history prepared for her, which I recited. She listened carefully, took notes, asked questions. To help me track down the cause of my bone loss, she ordered the

---

[7] Kaleta, M, et al. "The most common errors in the densitometric diagnosis of osteoporosis." *Ortopedia, traumatologia, rehabilitacja* vol.3,3 (2001): 338-44.. Accessed March 9, 2021.

ring ten tests:

- CBC with Differential/Platelet
- Metabolic Panel
- Sedimentation Rate-Westergren
- Thyroid
- Parathyroid
- 24-hour urine collection to test for bone breakdown/rapid bone turnover
- Celiac Disease
- N-Telopeptide
- Vitamin D level

These seemed to be comprehensive tests and I was relieved. I would finally get somewhere, would get the answers to these very troubling questions. While I waited for the results, I pondered these additional questions:

What was the level of "normal" to which my DEXA scans were compared?

Who manufactures DEXA machines? Do they profit from osteoporosis drugs?

I also went to a nutritionist in Princeton, New Jersey, to help ensure that my diet was giving me the best bang for my buck; in other words, was I absorbing enough calcium? How could I ensure that my diet was alkaline? I certainly was well-read and had already spent a lot of time reading about my circumstances and what steps I could take to answer these questions myself. Dr. DeFelice referred me to this nutritionist at my request. When I looked her up online, however, I saw that she appeared to be very young. I almost did not keep the appointment as I had already been disappointed in so many professional people in my life and had no desire to waste my time on an inexperienced, green nutritionist who was still wet behind the ears. But I did go, because I wanted to pursue every possibility.

Before my appointment with the nutritionist, my diet had continued to evolve. I started eating soy on August 9, 2015, since the evidence I found demonstrated that "a diet high in soy foods strengthens bone."[8] Dr. Lanou and Michael Castleman found thirty-one studies of soy foods' effect on bone density, much of it compelling and supportive of this conclusion.[9]

For example, one Vanderbilt University study showed that, as soy intake increased, fracture risk decreased.[10] That makes those soy "Chik'n" patties pretty attractive. And there are myriad soy products on the market. It's not just tofu anymore. There is soy milk, soy nuts, and edamame. Soy protein enhances a wide array of foods, including soy cheese, soy pasta, soy meat crumbles, and

---

[8] Lanou, Amy Joy et al. *building bone vitality*. McGraw Hill 2009, p 124.

[9] Ibid.
[10] Ibid., p. 125

soy protein bars.

At first, I went soy crazy. I bought veggie and soy burgers, soy "chicken" patties and nuggets, and tofu. I also kept chowing down heavily on all kinds of fruits and veggies, as well as dried fruit, since Dr. Lanou had likened raisins to "bone bullets" since "a couple of handfuls of raisins neutralize the acid produced by most animal foods."[11]

Raisins

Given the high fiber and roughage content of my diet, I also began to experience a different consequence than I had hoped for: I was constantly running to the toilet in the morning. And I mean running. As in, I had better get there in time or suffer the consequences.

This condition worsened and began to interfere with my life. I had trouble getting out the door to make the fifty-minute drive (on a good day) to my office. One morning, I had to stop five times on the way to work. My gut had become dysfunctional.

On September 24, 2015, when I saw the nutritionist, I almost said nothing about my GI issues. There was already enough to talk about to ensure I was eating right for my bones. But as I was holding my list of high calcium foods (seriously? I could have recited this list from memory, and even if I could not, I could have looked that up on the internet. For what reason did I

[11] Ibid., p.197

need a nutritionist?), it popped into my head and I told her.

She immediately started asking me a series of questions, as if she were going down a decision tree. I answered yes to every single one. She said, "Oh, we call that a stomach attack. You have IBS." She turned around, pulled out another sheet from her filing cabinet, and placed it on the desk between us. "You need to go on the FODMAP diet."

My mind started turning. Nutrition is one of my pet topics, but I knew next to nothing about the FODMAP diet. I had once read an article about it in Reader's Digest. That was the extent of my knowledge about FODMAPs. At the time, I remember thinking, "Oh, those poor people." Now I was one of those poor people.

I was already holding a handout showing the foods I needed to eat to stay alkaline to protect my skeleton. I compared the alkaline food list to the FODMAP list that the nutritionist had just handed to me. There was virtually no overlap.

Stricken, I looked up at the nutritionist. My mouth was probably hanging open in shock.

"What am I supposed to eat?" I asked her.

"Well," she said, squirming at the difficulty of answering this question, "an alkaline diet is often fish and vegetables." She said I could eat that on a FODMAP diet.

There were a few issues with that statement, however.

First, you cannot eat fish and vegetables for every meal.

Second, on a FODMAP diet, the vegetables are limited, especially when you first begin, as the consumer will likely have to eat mostly root vegetables to calm down their digestive system.

Third, actually, according to Dr. Lanou, fish is an acid-producing food and its consumption would have to be balanced with a whole lotta fruits and vegetables. This would be a no-no on a FODMAP diet.

After I arrived home at the end of that day, I was prepared to tackle these issues head on. I sat down with my lists, determined to find foods that would work for me. After combing the lists, however, I still could not find much that matched.

FODMAP is an acronym that stands for Fermentable Oligo-, Di-, and Monosaccharides and Polyols. The first foods to be axed from my diet were garlic and onion, which are two foods that are absolute must-not-consume high-FODMAP items. Gone were my daily apples, my bone bullet raisins. No more watermelon, cauliflower, beans, milk, wheat, hummus, honey. The list went on and on. Even many of the foods that were permitted on the low-FODMAP list were allowed only in very small quantities. I could eat broccoli, but only one-quarter of a cup.

Distressed, I read an article online by a brave nutritionist who had been diagnosed with IBS and placed on a low-FODMAP diet. While in the grocery store searching for food she was allowed to eat, she collapsed on the floor in tears. I could relate. I could not eat anything. Every food label contained at least one black-listed item (wheat, lactose, high-fructose corn syrup, garlic, onion). For those of you with celiac disease, you are already familiar with the way wheat is included in so many foods you would not expect at first (mustard, salad dressing, soup), and that companies sometimes hide its inclusion as "natural flavor" or some other impenetrable nonsense.

I finally made my pathetic list and, with tears in my eyes, forged onward to the supermarket. I bought eggs, cucumbers, gluten-free waffles, strawberries, sardines, gluten-free crackers, gluten-free pretzels, baby carrots, canned Alaskan salmon, and kefir.

I had never ingested kefir before, but I had heard of it. One of my great friends is from Moscow, and she drinks it all the time. It is a staple in Russian households. My FODMAP list permitted me to buy only one kind of kefir (the Russians say "keh FEER" instead of "KEFF er") by Lifeway. Lucky for me, my supermarket carried that brand with no flavoring or other added ingredients, which is required for the low-FODMAP diet.

Back home, with low-FODMAP items stowed and prepared to be carted off to the office the next day, I downed a glass of kefir. I held my nose, but I swallowed it. To my amazement, even before I opened my eyes the next morning, I felt the difference in my gut. It was calm and quiet. It felt great. I believe that the immediate change was due to the alteration in my diet the previous day and the probiotic effect of the kefir .

Thus began a months-long quest to get my gut back in order while continuing to be on an absolute panic-driven mission to stop my avalanche of bone loss and, instead, to increase my bone density. From a general perspective, I have always been a weird food eater. That is, I ate a healthy diet virtually all of the time. My family, my friends, and my colleagues often commented about my food choices. Now, however, my eating regime had gone way beyond the pale of normalcy. For breakfast, I would eat egg whites and cucumbers. For lunch, I would have sardines, a food I had neither eaten nor craved before, and Nut Thins gluten-free crackers with raw carrots.

It was confusing. Some websites said you could eat banana on a FODMAP diet. Others said, no, only if they were green. Even though I like my bananas well-done (with lots of brown dots so their sweetness is well-developed), I tried eating a fully green banana. Yuk. It was like eating a bamboo pole. Not worth it.

I alternated my focus between bones and gut.

For the Bones: Keep walking. Yoga twice per week. Targeted weight training. Consider a trainer. Sit less. Consume leafy greens, sea vegetables (seaweed), foods rich in potassium and magnesium and calcium and phytoestrogens (whole grain barley, rice, oats, linseed or flaxseed, sunflower, anise, sesame, green and yellow vegetables, carrots, beet greens, bok choy, collards). Also consider consuming:

- 1 tablespoon blackstrap molasses, okra, rhubarb, turnip greens
- No caffeine
- Vitamin D
- 350-600 mg buffered magnesium
- Calcium 1200-1500 mg per day, found in green leafy vegetables, seeds, and seaweed
- Vitamin K 45 mg per day
- Manganese RDA 15-20 mg, found in pecans, peanuts, oatmeal, rice, and sweet potato
- Zinc 10-30 mg daily, found in pumpkin seeds
- Copper 3 mg daily to prevent bone loss, found in leafy greens, and grains
- Strontium 1-3 mg
- Boron 2-6 mg, found in sea vegetables, leafy vegetables, avocadoes, and nuts
- Silicon, found in hard unprocessed grains and vegetables, cabbage, parsnips, and radishes

- Betaine
- Folic Acid, B6, B12, found in green leafy vegetables, citrus, and whole grain cereal
- Vitamin A and C, but with a warning to keep the Vitamin A low, as some sources indicate it may increase hip fracture[12]
- Vitamin E, found in sunflower seeds and almonds
- Essential Fatty Acids, found in fish oil and primrose oil, with an increase in BMD when used together.

Once I returned from a holiday in October 2015, I started using all of these vitamins and minerals daily. The actual start date was October 18, 2015.

On October 26, 2015, I added a whole egg (versus an egg white) to support cognitive function per suggestion of George Gallop[13], owner of my local health food store in New Jersey. Mr. Gallop had spent a lifetime learning about good nutrition. He and I had had some stimulating discussions in the past and I believed him to be quite knowledgeable.

On November 14, 2015, I realized that cucumbers are not the magic alkalizers I thought they were. I also realized

---

[12] Sanson, Gillian. *The Myth of Osteoporosis*. MCD Century Publications, LLC. 2003, Revised 2011. P. 159. First accessed 2015; accessed again December 11, 2020.
[13] His name is changed to protect his privacy.

that my nutritionist had given me misinformation about what foods create an alkaline environment in the body. The handout she had given me was from the Alkaline Sisters website, but at least some of the information therein was incorrect. Dr. Lanou has the actual source on pages 56 and 60 of her book, *building bone vitality*. Once I discovered this, I had to rethink what to eat to create low alkalinity while I adhered to a low FODMAP diet. I decided to introduce one ounce of raisins—the bone bullets—to see if I could tolerate them gastrointestinally. The raisins would reduce the overall score of acid/alkalinity by -5.2. Pretty solid. By comparison, cucumbers provided a balance of only -0.8.

I found an online source called Gout Pal to help me estimate my potential renal acid load, or PRAL. The target was to create a thirty percent (30%) acid to seventy percent (70%) alkaline environment, demonstrated by a final score of a negative number. I began testing my pH level and found it in the right place: 6.25, 7.25, 6.5, 6.5.

Breakfast:	
6 ox Fage 0% yogurt approximately	-0.54*
3 oz almonds	-0.19
Banana	-6.93
Blueberries	-1.04
Tea	-.81
With lemon	-.3
Total	-9.81

In case you run into this difficulty (and I fervently hope you do not), here are some sample alkaline/ FODMAP diet plans which include a calculation of PRAL:

*Although Fage is a good yogurt, I started eating Siggi's as recommended by a low-FODMAP plan I found. I later stopped eating yogurt at all for a while, and have come back full circle to Fage.

Lunch:	
4 oz FODMAP Friendly BBQ chicken per 100 g	+15.58
Yam per 100 g	-12.17
Zucchini in tomato puree, 7 oz	-9.52[14]
Raisins, 1 oz	-3.42
Total	**-9.53**

Dinner:	
Gluten Free Bagel	+5.58
Almond Butter	-0.56
1 oz raisins	-3.42
Zucchini in tomato sauce	-9.52
Total	**-7.92**

My GI system was in pretty good shape during the Fall of 2015, and I was doing everything I could do to increase my bone density. I continued to read everything I could on the subject and to search for answers. After

---

[14] -4.76 per 100 g, so 100 g = 3.53 oz, 1 g = 0.0353 oz

eight weeks on a strict FODMAP diet, I slowly started adding in some foods that had been prohibited, including Greek yogurt and raisins.

Meanwhile, life continued, and my husband had a Total Hip Replacement (THR) of his right hip at Hospital for Special Surgery in New York City on November 18, 2015. The surgery and initial recovery went very well and I brought him home on Saturday morning, November 21. I could have driven him home the day before, in the afternoon, but such a drive was prohibitive in rush hour traffic.

We had Thanksgiving Dinner at our home on November 26, 2015. Later that day, my GI symptoms began to return. I had a lot of bloating, gas, and other IBS symptoms. This continued all weekend, so I scheduled an appointment with my internist on December 1. He said there was no need for medication or other tests and that I should eat a "commonsense diet." Despite the commonsense diet (I think I had already been eating a commonsense diet anyway), the symptoms continued, so next I scheduled to see my gastroenterologist. He couldn't see me until December 16, 2015, two weeks later. I had prepared for the appointment in advance by drafting the following pertinent points, and the progression, of my condition:

- About seven years earlier, I had had an episode of a sudden attack of horrendous diarrhea. My internist told me at the time that I had had food poisoning from eating unwashed greens at a boardwalk restaurant at the Jersey Shore.

- Since then, I had suffered occasional "stomach attacks" where I would have to run for the toilet.

- A couple of years earlier, the same gastroenterologist had voiced his opinion that I had IBS.

- My condition grew worse in the Spring of 2013 after several intensely stressful months. I was handling my usual heavy litigation case load plus fifty percent of the case load of one of my attorneys who was on maternity leave. In addition, I had been very ill with some type of respiratory illness for the entire month of March and, despite the illness, had two business trips out of state. I became very run down and ended up with shingles, which appeared at the end of the month.

- I tried numerous interventions, including psychotherapy and Xanax. I would normally reject a psychopharmacologic medication, but I told myself I had better be open-minded and try it. For me, it was ineffective.

- After I received the dire news of my increased bone loss on June 1, 2015, I went on a low acid diet, mostly vegan, including beans. After a few months, this exacerbated the stomach attacks. I had trouble getting out of the house every morning because I could not leave the toilet. I began to wear a diaper for the trip to work.

- On September 23, 2015, I saw a nutritionist. We discussed the low FODMAP diet, kefir, and a critical care probiotic.

- I immediately started using these items and saw an immediate overnight change.

- I had six weeks of strict adherence on the FODMAP diet with a few slight hitches because I made a mistake in the eating regimen. After that time, I did as recommended and added other food items: Greek yogurt, a few raisins, and other items.

- While staying in a guest suite during my husband's total hip replacement, on November 18, 2015, I had some kind of vasovagal response with strong discomfort before I passed a stool with sweating, nausea, and as if my guts needed to get rid of something that was in there which was not coming out.

- Upon returning home from the hospital on Saturday, November 21, 2015, I had a sore throat, a cough, was tired, and felt ill.

- On Wednesday, November 24, 2015, I felt bloated and gassy.

- On Thanksgiving, I ate some extra foods I had been avoiding, including one and one-half glasses of white wine, two really small bites of sweet potato pie (no crust, so no wheat), green beans in stock with possible garlic flavor and cranberry sauce. Afterward, I felt gassy, had an achy tummy, increased stools throughout the day and also on Friday, Saturday, and Sunday . I kept running to the toilet.

- I ate a really restricted diet on November 30, had Pepto Bismol at 7 am and again at 12:30-ish. I felt better, but not normal.

- I called the internist on November 30 and was referred to the GI doctor.

- Meanwhile, I tried to eat the commonsense diet and looked up more info on treating IBS .

At my meeting with the GI doctor, I shared those points with him quickly and succinctly, including that I was on a low-FODMAP diet. He basically repeated back to me what I had told him: he diagnosed me with IBS-D subsequent to food poisoning. He told me I could stick to the low-FODMAP diet, although he remarked, "That's a really tough diet to follow," and he prescribed me a two-week trial of Xifaxin and Hyocyamine as needed. He also advised that he would schedule me for a colonoscopy if the medication did not help. On the way out of the office, I made an appointment for the colonoscopy in case I needed it. Although it was only mid-December, the procedure was not scheduled until mid-February.

Unfortunately, the Xifaxin had absolutely no effect on my GI symptoms. In fact, they seemed worse, and I had a lot of stomach pain and distress. I ordered some peppermint essential oil and applied it directly to my abdomen when I had stomach pain. That helped more than the Xifaxin. I read up on different organisms that can live in the gut and cause these symptoms. I called my GI's office and asked to be tested. After some back-and-forth phone discussion with the staff, and the staff with the doctor, they agreed to do a few tests. The ones they agreed to do came back negative. I returned to a strict low-FODMAP diet as of December 31, 2015.

The low-FODMAP diet was developed by a research team at Monash University in Melbourne, Australia. The team included a woman named Sue Shepherd. Her Ph.D research and other work demonstrated that FODMAPs could trigger IBS, and consequently, a low-FODMAP diet was an effective treatment for those symptoms. More information can be found at shepherdworks.com.au as well as en.m.wikipedia.org. Phase 1 involves strict restriction of all high-FODMAP foods for 4-6 weeks. Phase 2 is the gradual reintroduction of restricted foods to see what the individual can tolerate. Everyone has different food tolerances. Shepherd Works strongly recommends consultation with an experienced dietitian during all aspects of the low-FODMAP diet.

My recovery was not as quick this time around. I had diarrhea every morning again from November 30 into

January and had to wear a diaper in order to drive all the way to my office, a 50-minute drive. The diarrhea was uncontrollable at times. I have had to strip down in the public office bathroom multiple times to wash up before my work day started. Luckily, I was an early bird and therefore there was no one else in the building, so I had privacy. I would often not eat breakfast for fear of another episode. I kept reading more about IBS and the low-FODMAP diet and kept changing the foods I was eating. Nothing was helping. I started taking Pepto Bismol regularly. It was a difficult time and I felt alone and responsible for solving these issues by myself. But this was intolerable and I knew I could not continue to live that way. I needed help.

I tried to find a dietician or nutritionist familiar with the FODMAP diet. I called a few people who looked promising, but no one really knew what I was talking about. I was willing to travel, as usual, but even by widening my search, there was no help to be found. I found a nutritionist 45 minutes from my home who was also a registered nurse, but even she told me she did not have the knowledge to help me.

Meanwhile, I stuck to the FODMAP diet. It was very limiting and the results were unpredictable. I kept reading and learning more as I went along. I love fruit and vegetables, but did not eat as much as I used to. I ate mostly eggs, chicken, root vegetables, and gluten-free bagels . Breakfast was usually pretty weird. Can you imagine eating a baked yam, two egg whites, and blueberries for breakfast? And sardines on Nut Thins crackers with cucumbers for lunch? Sardines are not my favorite; in fact, I had never eaten them before. Not something I found enticing. But necessity dictates action. Despite all my efforts, the stomach pain and diarrhea continued. My stomach at times felt "trashed," uneasy, bilious .

As the date of my colonoscopy neared, my symptoms began to lessen, but did not completely subside. I debated whether to have it done. I really did not want to undergo the procedure, but I determined to go through with it because it might yield the answer to my GI trouble.

My February 10, 2016 colonoscopy went off without a hitch. The diagnosis showed colonic mucosa with no diagnostic abnormalities. No lymphocytic or collagenous colitis was identified. That was great news, but shed no light on my egregious GI issues. The colonoscopy discharge papers advised me to eat a high fiber diet.

For about a week and a half after the colonoscopy, I had wicked, smelly gas. I took a lot of Pepto Bismol to help control the symptoms. It is hard to work with clients and co-workers if you are farting up a smelly storm. It finally went away. On February 25 and 26, respectively, I had normal stools and hoped that I was finally healthy and healing. On February 26, I was so couraged that I was daring in the afternoon and had a snack of red grapes on an empty stomach. March 3, 2016 was the first day since November 23, 2015 I felt comfortable enough to make my morning commute to work without wearing a diaper. *Hooray for the FODMAP diet*, I thought. It is hard to feel sexy or feminine when you are wearing a diaper and not sure when your bowels are about to give way.

During all of this GI fun I was having, I was of course still in a panic about my bones. Add that to balancing my ever-demanding litigation career. I am sure that the steady panic and stress had a negative effect on my gut and my bones.

It occurred to me that one way to increase my bone density would be to engage in targeted exercise as opposed to *all* the varied exercise I always did and still do. At that point, instead of finding or creating my own exercise regimen, I called my doctor's office to ask if I could have a referral to physical therapy. The doctor immediately wrote a script, which left me wondering why he had not referred me to PT on June 1, 2015, when I asked him what else I could do to increase my bone density.

I started PT immediately. I got a great set of exercises targeting my hips, the site of my bone loss. They certainly felt effective. I did three sets of wall-ankle pushes, bridges with TheraBand, bridges with leg lift, and clamshells *every single day*.

After I had been to see the nutritionist, I returned to Dr. DeFelice for follow-up after my lab work. We discussed the test results, and she proposed to put me on a bone density drug. After her proposal, I said, "Let's talk about that," and I stated the knowledge I had gained about each of the drugs and drug categories. I listed the benefits of each as well as the potential side effects. Moreover, I noted the risks of osteosarcoma, necrosis of the jaw, premature fracture of the femur, and esophageal cancer. I finished by saying that the bone built with some of the medications tends to be brittle bone and more likely to fracture, and asked, "Isn't that what we are trying to prevent?" My goal there was to tell her what I had already learned and then ask her to give me more information from her knowledge and experience so I could sift through and consider facts to which I was not already privy. Instead, she sat in silence, then admitted she did not know the answer to that question. She told me that she would be following me to see what I would do. I later learned that most physicians cannot keep up-to-date on all of the drugs being produced and introduced, and therefore they rely on something like Cliff's Notes for physicians: certain physicians will read up on the new medications and send out brief synopses of the drugs. Apparently, these synopses did not contain the answers to my questions.

Since I had not gotten much help from the physicians

I had already seen, upon the advice of my dentist, who strongly advised I not take bisphosphonates, I then sought out the opinion of an endocrinologist. I drove an hour from my office, which is almost an hour from my home in the opposite direction, to the best endocrinologist I could find in the entire state of New Jersey.

The morning of the appointment, May 11, 2016, I was at my office when my law partner, Staci, told me she had been referred to a new physician by one of our experts. The expert, a neuropsychologist, had expressed how much she respected, trusted, and believed in this doctor, and urged us to see her as well.

I did not know it then, but that referral was the start of healing for my GI system, and for my whole self as well.

I arrived at the endocrinologist's office early, so I contacted the newly-referred physician, Dr. Isabella Franzese. The office advised me she was not seeing new patients but had a Nurse Practitioner with whom she worked closely, and the NP could see me. I took the insurance codes from the staff and advised I would call them back once I found out if my insurance would cover the visit. Then I went inside to see the endocrinologist.

She was very professional and I liked her a lot. She sat down with me in the examining room and took a history from me. I explained I had been diagnosed with osteoporosis and my bones were thinning at an alarming rate. That calcium and vitamin D supplements had not helped. That I had been aware since I was 23 years of age that I had several risk factors for the development of osteoporosis: female, small frame, Caucasian, light weight. And that I had taken great care all my life to develop and live a lifestyle conducive to maintaining a healthy bone structure: intense exercise, running, weight lifting, good diet, addition of extra calcium to my diet by adding dried milk to my tea, but that back issues around the time of menopause caused me to drastically reduce weightlifting and turn instead to yoga. I told her about my poor DEXA scan from the previous June, the literature review and change of diet, Dr. Amy Lanou and her theory of RAL—Renal Acid Load—and its effect on the skeleton, that I had changed other factors, including walking every day for 30-60 minutes, using a stand up and walk desk, low acid diet, continued weight lifting, physical therapy to target bones and hips, striving for less stress and more balance in my life, and had gotten a second opinion from a rheumatologist. I also told her my mother had had parathyroid issues and had two of those glands removed at age 83.

I told the endocrinologist that I wanted her opinion as to what was causing the osteoporosis and what else I could do about it. I wanted her thoughts on Forteo: Did she think it reduced the FRAX risk significantly? And I wanted her thoughts on my concern about balancing that and the increased risk for osteosarcoma. I told her I wanted to look at my biochemical bone markers, my thyroid function, and my parathyroid function. I told her I had intense pressure in my abdomen early in the morning, around 4:30 to 5 am with a drawing sensation from the head and wanted to determine what was causing it. Was it low blood glucose? It was strong enough that it woke me up and made me feel strange and uncomfortable.

I had prepared for this meeting by studying my risk of fracture and comparing that with the risk of drug and the reduction of the fracture risk. Here's what I found:

My overall fracture risk at the time was 11%.

My hip fracture risk was 3.9%.

The use of <u>Fosomax</u> at 10 mg for three years would provide:

- 53% decrease in chance of hip fracture
- Increase in bone density by 13.7% at the lumbar spine, 10.3% at the trochanter, 5.4% at the femoral neck, and 6.7% at the total proximal femur.[15]
- Hip BMD would remain stable, but maintained

---

[15] Bone, Henry G., MD et al. "Ten Years' Experience with Alendronate for Osteoporosis in Postmenopausal Women." *N Engl J Med* 2004; 350:1189-1199. Doi:10.1056/NE/Moa030897. Accessed February 25, 2021.

at 5-7% above baseline

- No difference in fracture rate between those who stopped taking Fosomax and those who continued taking Fosomax.
- Safety: common symptoms included heartburn, stomach pain, diarrhea, muscle and joint pain, and non-healing sores
- After two years of treatment, the average BMD increases included 7% in the lumbar spine, 3.5% in the total hip, and 3% in the femoral neck.
- The risk of esophageal cancer doubled to 2 in 1,000 users.

[handwritten margin note: Jaw deterioration of bone]

The use of <u>Forteo</u> would yield:

- Reduction of fracture:

  - Spine   65%
  - Nonspine   53%
  - Hip   Too few to count

- Risk of osteosarcoma
- Use limited to two years in a lifetime
- Leg cramping, reduced blood pressure
- After 19 months, BMD increases were:

  - Lumbar spine   9.7%
  - Total hip   2.6%
  - Femoral neck   2.8%

- But bone density rapidly decreases after

cessation. Forteo is not effective in reducing fracture risk in hip.[16]

- Bisphosphonates stay in the bone.
- Seems to be indicated for those with low spine density and at high risk for fractures or for those who have already sustained spinal fracture.

The endocrinologist looked over my medical records, which I had sent to her in advance. She advised that bone density peaks at 35 years of age, and after menopause, a bone loss of two percent or more annually is normal. My most recent medical testing showed no multiple myeloma. My pituitary function was normal. My urine NTX—the marker of bone turnover—was at the higher end of normal. The endocrinologist was not sure why. She surmised that I might not have reached peak bone mass at 35. But I had no celiac marker. My calcium was normal. Ultimately, the endocrinologist agreed that the tests I had requested were appropriate. She planned to do a 24-hour urine calcium and a repeat 24-hour urine. It was important to know the volume and to have creatinine results. She would also test my vitamin D levels, test for Cushing syndrome, which would cause over-secretion of cortisol and adrenal insufficiency.

---

[16] Schneider, Diane L. MD. *The Complete Book of Bone Health*. Prometheus Books. New York. 2011, p.236. Accessed February 25, 2021.

I asked her about my Z scores, since those are DEXA scores compared to my same-age peers, whe the T scores are compared to younger women. My spine showed osteopenia, meaning anything lower than -1.5. Mine was -1.9. When we compared my May 2013 DEXA to my May 2015 DEXA, my spine showed no statistically significant loss. My hips were of greater *my Aches* concern, however. My T score was -3.4 and my Z score was -2.4. My left hip was worse, she said, and was questionable as it appeared to be an excessive rate of bone loss. I had experienced six to seven percent loss instead of the four or five percent that would have been expected in those two years.

As a precautionary measure, she advised I should not do high-risk activities like skiing or horseback riding. That was bad enough, but she added that, when it was snowing, I should use crampons to walk on the ice. Do not go up ladders, she advised. I felt like an old lady.

She said she would definitely treat me. She talked about the potential medications. "Forteo is a very good drug," she said, "but they save that for last. It is very effective, but it comes with 'Black Box Warnings' that 1 in 400,000 people who use it come down with osteosarcoma." *Tell me something I don't already know*, I thought.

She would start with a bisphosphonate. *Fosamax* However, some consumers developed osteonecrosis in the jaw.

This happened to only a low percentage and usually in patients who had already had cancers. I asked her about the literature on bisphosphonates which says the bone developed in its use is spongy bone, and that consumers can develop esophageal cancers. True, she said. The quality of bone is an issue, but she advised it did decrease the FRAX score and it did increase bone mineral density. The use of bisphosphonates must be stopped after four years, though, and she said the bone remains stable for only one year.

Prolia or Denosumab is another drug used to increase BMD. She said it gets really great results in BMD, and that patients continue to see increases for years. It is injected into the body every six months. The side effects do not last that long. There is an increased risk of cellulitis, usually for those on immunosuppressants.

Quite honestly, I was discouraged when I left that appointment. I had been fighting a lonely battle for almost a year. Every physician I had consulted had recommended medication. I had been unable to find any real expert on osteoporosis who recommended anything else. It was wearing me down.

But I was not ready to give in. Not yet. I had made up my mind. I would have another DEXA scan, and I would see if any of the interventions I had undertaken had been effective.

It was all very frightening.

The Monday after I saw the endocrinologist, I contacted my insurance to see if they would cover a visit to Dr. Isabella Franzese. They would. I then looked at Dr. Franzese's website. I liked what I saw. She had stellar credentials, but the narrative touted her integration of natural medicine with traditional medical practices, homeopathy, nutrition, and acupuncture. She treats the whole patient. Intrigued and hopeful, I called the office to make an appointment with the Nurse Practitioner. While they had me on the line to do so, I heard the receptionist gasp and say, "This never happens! Hold on," she said, and put me on hold. She came back right away and said, "Someone canceled and Dr. Franzese actually has an opening for a new patient."

"That's great," I answered. "When is it?" I held my breath. My schedule as a litigation attorney was wicked and unforgiving.

She replied, "It's for tomorrow."

EUREKA! FIREWORKS! UNBELIEVABLE!

She was right. This never happens. At least, not to me.

Until it did. For complicated reasons, I actually had the entire next day cleared to work at home, with no phone conferences, consultations, meetings, mediations, or court appearances. I had never had a day like that before in my entire career. Except for the following day. Exactly when Dr. Franzese had the rare opening.

"I'll take it."

Thus began a very fortuitous relationship that was the next leg of this incredible journey.

Dr. Franzese's office was over an hour away, straight up the New Jersey Turnpike, the last exit before the George Washington Bridge. I had to be there at 8:00 am for bloodwork the next morning. Since I lived at the Jersey Shore in Central New Jersey and I knew I would have a lot of company on the turnpike, I left the house at 6 am. Better safe than sorry. I did not want to cut it close and arrive in a sweat, or worse, get stuck in a commuter traffic jam and miss the coveted appointment altogether. I arrived on time, had eighteen vials of my blood drawn, peed in a cup, and returned two weeks later for my appointment with Dr. Franzese.

This doctor visit and examination was like nothing else I had ever experienced in my life. Dr. Franzese's office seemed to have positive chi or energy. The staff were friendly and welcoming. The furniture was comfortable and made out of natural materials. The atmosphere was not sterile or impersonal. Rather, there were artful messages of encouragement adorning the walls and green leafy plants gave the room life and vitality.

After meeting with the nurse to go over my history and obtain my vitals, I met with Dr. Franzese in her office. The air of coziness carried over here. I felt a strange mixture of anticipatory trepidation given the gravity of my situation as well as a curious, almost supernatural calm born of the knowledge that I was in the right place at the right time.

Dr. Franzese's medical credentials were impeccable, but she also brought Eastern medicine and alternative medicine into her practice. During that first appointment, she mentioned the contrast of Western medicine, which employs medicine and techniques to block processes in the body, to Eastern medicine, which seeks to free up flow in the body and to unleash the body's natural healing power. She focused a great deal on nutrition, unlike any doctor I had ever met in my fifty-five years, and she used natural supplements, vitamins, and minerals to support the body's healing processes.

After talking about my presenting problems and looking over my medical history, Dr. Franzese performed the normal tasks one would expect at a physician appointment: she listened to my heart and lungs, looked in my eyes, ears, nose, and mouth. She had me lie down on the examining table and pressed down in various spots. She had me sit up and tested my reflexes with the reflex hammer. Then she did something that changed everything.

Dr. Franzese had me stand up and face the other way. She made me extend my arms out to the side, then hold them firmly and told me to resist her attempts to force them down. Then she repeatedly used her fingers to write on my back, then attempted to force my arm to my side. At times, I was able to resist her; at other times, I seemed to have no strength in my arm and she moved it down easily.

The first time it happened, I said, "Wait, wait, I wasn't ready." I thought she was able to force my arm down because I hadn't had a warning and didn't stiffen up my arm in time. Dr. Franzese chuckled quietly and said, "That's not how it works. I'm asking your body what it needs, and it's telling me. Bodies are smart and they know what they need."

After one gentle writing on my back and pushing my arm down, Dr. Franzese paused a moment. I waited. She then announced, "It's okay to take a step back and do less."

Bam! Those words pierced my heart like an arrow and freed years of stifled feelings which came pouring out. It was painful and beautiful and literally awesome and freeing. At the time, I really did not understand the full import of what had happened in that moment. I was too busy taking it all in and feeling it, sensing it. I turned to her and exclaimed, "What is that? What are you doing? It's like a mixture of doctoring and psychotherapy and witchcraft." I'm sure my eyes widened in response to my own words spoken aloud. I am not the type to blurt something out, especially if it might hurt someone else's feelings. I was brought up to think of others first, and I have always done that. I have had to learn to think of myself. But this just burst out of my mouth in that overwhelming, unusual moment.

But Dr. Franzese merely chuckled again. "It's called Applied Kinesiology. I'm asking your body what it needs and what's good for it." She continued doing this and making notes on her laptop, then we sat down and she proceeded to share with me the types of supplements she wanted me to take. I left her office with a prescription for a DEXA scan so we could see what my skeleton had been doing for the last year. I left Dr. Franzese's office with hope and the seed of painful but joyful new growth planted.

About three weeks later, I was preparing to leave the house about 6:15 in the morning for my hour drive to the office. Before I walked into the garage, I checked my email and saw one from Dr. Franzese telling me the results of my DEXA scan were in and I could view them in her online portal.

Can you imagine, dear Reader, the fear and trepidation I suddenly felt? Here I was, exactly one year after getting some of the scariest news of my life: that my bones had been disappearing at an alarming rate. Had they continued to disappear? After fighting a lonely battle for twelve months, after several highly-regarded doctors told me I needed to go on medication, I was to find out whether my own interventions had any difference in my bone density. Who was I to contradict modern medicine and multiple experienced physicians?

It was a stark moment of reckoning.

But I had to know. I signed into the portal and opened up the DEXA scan report. I began reading, my eyes scanning the page, fairly bouncing down the lines, driven by a fight-or-flight response. Looking, looking. Then I saw it. I read these words, but it was hard to wrap my head around it. The report in pertinent part read, "Mild osteoporosis left femoral neck with statistically significant 11.3% interval improvement since prior DEXA 5-19-05(sic—the date was really 5-19-15)."

I was stunned into silence. Could I really believe what I was reading? I had stabilized the bone loss in my entire hip and had improved the bone density in my left femoral neck, the area of most danger, called Ward's Triangle, the one most likely to fracture—by a "statistically significant 11.3%." Incredible! Amazing! I had done it, by myself, rejecting the medicine that doctors had tried to prescribe for me. I was elated.

The work was not over yet, though, by any means. You see, bone is living tissue, and the body continues to absorb and to re-build it. The fun never ends. But at least now I knew I could do it, and I knew how to do it.

Moreover, my spine had not had the same imp
I had wrought in my left femoral neck. I had
forward.

Dear Reader, right about now, you may be wanting
to find out my secret to success, the silver bullet that
neutralizes the deadly threat of osteoporosis. The
answer to that question is complicated. Modern
medicine holds that thinning bones are a natural part of
aging.[17] Too much thinning, however, may be caused by
individual circumstances. Pay close attention to the
information in this book so you will be able to pinpoint
your risk factors and to determine which interventions
are right for you. These details are the tools that you will
need to use to increase your own bone density.

I still had work to do, as do you. The next part of my
journey was different, though. I now had a powerful
ally: a physician who believed in natural interventions,
methods which would support the body's natural
processes and flow, but which were grounded in solid
data and research. I had some things to learn from Dr.
Franzese, and she, in turn, learned some things from me.

After I learned that I had increased my bone density
by a whopping 11.3%, I was plagued by the thought of
all the men and women in the USA, indeed, in the entire
world, who were taking medication to increase their
bone density. Had they been offered more conservative,

---

[17] This is not true across all cultures.

non-medicinal interventions? After my own experiences, I thought not. I tossed and turned in my bed at night, sleepless, imagining how I could reach all of those people. I pictured myself renting out hotel conference rooms, meeting in small home groups, holding presentations in libraries, just to tell these men and women how I increased my own bone density. If I had done it, I knew they could do it, too.

I worked up a business plan, opened a limited liability corporation, and ordered business cards. Practicalities and priorities presented themselves, however. I already had a full-time job, one that demanded many hours of every day. When I wasn't at work, I often took phone calls from clients and answered their emails. I was also busy writing my second novel, a project which I eventually had to shelve. I had hit a dead end. I simply had no time to devote to spreading the word in the fight against osteopenia and osteoporosis, as much as I wanted to do it.

Fast forward five and a half years. Dr. Franzese is still my doctor. Prior to writing this book, I published three others: The Handbook for Parents of Children with Special Needs: A Therapeutic and Legal Approach; Hurts So Good: An Orgasm of Tears; and the Hurts So Good: An Orgasm of Tears Workbook. I still work hard every day to grow and strengthen my bones. I get tired of it some days. I feel discouraged by the sheer and steady need of my bones. But, like the Tubthumping

Chumbawamba's, I get knocked down, but I get up again. And you're never gonna keep me down.

If you are scared because your bones are thinning and you don't know what to do, I understand. I have been where you are standing. If you have tried so hard, eaten well, taken your calcium and vitamin D supplements, and are discouraged because it's not working, I hear you. I have felt that fear, that discouragement, that pain.

But I am writing this book to tell you, yes, you, dear Reader, that you can increase your bone density with a careful evaluation of your lifestyle and some adjustments to it. ***Essentially, this is the silver bullet.*** You and your trusted physician will assess, intervene on behalf of, and monitor your bones as I describe in the upcoming chapters. It doesn't matter whether or not you are taking FDA-approved medications to treat your osteopenia or your osteoporosis. You can employ these strategies and interventions. If I can do it, you can do it, too. This is how you can slow, stop, and even reverse the thinning of your bones. Read on to discover the keys to building your bones.

Chapter Three
Assess Your Risk Factors

Factors That Cause Bones To Thin

Scientific research studies and the collection of relevant data have identified a number of factors which predispose humans to develop osteopenia and osteoporosis. They include:

1. Gender
2. Age
3. Small Frame
4. Tall Frame
5. Smoking
6. Sedentary Lifestyle
7. Lack of Exercise
8. Poor Nutrition
9. Alcohol Consumption
10. Steroid Use
11. Low Body Weight
12. Carbonated Cola Beverages
13. Lack of Sunshine

While any one of these factors can have an effect, a combination of four or more factors can put your bones into a vulnerable state vis-à-vis your bone density. Let us consider the causation behind each factor.

1. Gender. Women are more likely than men to develop osteopenia and osteoporosis. Here, biology is destiny. On average, women have smaller skeletons. All of their bones are smaller. Thus, their peak bone mass will decline from a thinner starting point.

2. Age. As humans age, our bones thin. This is not disease; it is a natural aging process. The older you get, the more your bones thin. The more your bones thin, the more likely they are to fracture.

3. Small frame. People who start out in life with a small skeleton are more likely to develop osteopenia and osteoporosis as their bones thin.

4. People whose height exceeds 5'8" are at risk because, if and when they fall, they are more likely to fracture a bone as the impact from the fall will be greater.

5. Smoking depletes the body of important vitamins and minerals and has a significant impact on bone health.

6. Sedentary Lifestyle. People who sit more than four hours per day are at greater risk for thinning bones. The body needs to bear its own weight in order for the bones to stay dense. When the skeleton is not asked to do this work, the bones react accordingly by growing ever thinner.

7. Lack of Exercise. While this factor may seem identical

to #6, Sedentary Lifestyle, it is not. In order to stay strong, bones need to be worked. In performing any type of weight-bearing exercise, the muscles push and pull on the bones. Called mechanical loading, which in turn causes mechanical strain, this type of demand spurs the bone cells called osteoblasts, which build new bone. In the absence of such demand, the osteoclasts do more work than the osteoblasts, thereby breaking down bone faster than the body builds it.

8. Poor Nutrition. The body needs a variety of vitamins and minerals to build bone. When we fail to eat a variety of foods and do not take appropriate supplements, our bodies simply do not have the ingredients with which to form new bone.

9. Alcohol Consumption. Studies show that heavy drinking increases your risk of fracturing your bones for a number of reasons. It suppresses the osteoblasts, or bone-building cells. It is linked with poor nutrition and smoking. It also impairs judgment and balance, increasing the risk of falling, a no-no all on its own. With all of its risks, however, a minority of other studies demonstrate that moderate alcohol consumption helps prevent fractures. Therefore, while there are mixed results, the studies suggest that those who enjoy an alcoholic drink should limit their consumption to no more than one to two drinks per day.

10. Steroid Use. Steroids suppress the work of osteoblasts,

the bone-building cells, and increase the rate at which bones are broken down. Studies show that long-term use is associated with fracture. Postmenopausal women who take steroids regularly have a very high risk of suffering a spinal fracture.

11. Low Body Weight. A body weight under 127 pounds increases your risk of low bone density and fracture. When you are a lightweight, the demand for weightbearing is less, and therefore, your bones are required to support less weight. As a result, there is less mechanical load, less strain on the bones, and they do not develop as much density. In addition, if a person with less cushioning around the bones, especially the hips, falls, they are more likely to experience a fracture.

12. Carbonated Beverages. Studies show that women who regularly drink cola-based soda have lower bone density and that adolescent girls who drink carbonated beverages have increased risk for low bone density and fractures. Further studies have been mixed, and some researchers believe that clear carbonated beverages do not deplete the body's bone density so long as you maintain your intake of appropriate vitamins and minerals.

13. Lack of Sunshine. When skin is exposed to sunlight, the body develops vitamin D. Vitamin D has several important functions, including the regulation of calcium for the normal growth and development of the skeleton. Therefore, a lack of sunshine precludes

production of vitamin D, which can place the skeleton in a vulnerable position.

Remember that one risk factor alone is unlikely to make a significant difference, but a combination of factors can put you at greater and greater risk. Use the list below to idenitfy your risk factors and review them objectively. Then read on for how to address the risks.[18]

What Is Your Risk?

The risk factors for osteopenia, osteoporosis, and subsequent bone fracture are listed below. Check off the ones which pertain to you.

1. Diabetes Mellitus   _____
2. Low Body Mass Index (under 127 lbs.)   _____
3. High salt diet   _____
4. Caffeine, esp coffee (2+ [tea, 4 +])   _____
5. Excess alcohol consumption (3+/day)   _____
6. Smoking   _____
7. Depression, anxiety, high cortisol   _____
8. Prescription drugs (tranquilizers, sedatives, Avandia, Actos, steroids, anticonvulsant, antacids and heartburn meds [Prilosec, Nexium, Prevacid], Aromatase inhibitors, Tamoxifen)   ✓_____
9. Age (postmenopausal +)   ✓_____
10. Female   ✓_____

---

[18] If you would like to read more about how the body breaks down and builds bone, please see the suggested reading list in Appendix A.

11. Caucasian   ✓ _____
12. Previous fracture   _____
13. Height (5'8"-fall farther)   _____
14. Family history of fracture   ✓ _____
15. Other illness   _____
16. Falls   _____
17. Insufficient vitamin D levels   _____
18. Removal of small intestine   _____
19. Poor nutrition   _____
20. Weight loss   _____
21. Sit more than 4 hours/day   _____
22. Less than 15 mins sunshine/day   _____

What Is Your FRAX Score?

You may or may not already know your FRAX score. Chances are, you don't. Not one of my physicians—and I had many that first year—explained this to me. For those of you who know it, you can skip this section. For those of you who don't, I will explain it briefly.

The FRAX (Fracture Risk Assessment Tool) was developed by the University of Sheffield and is used with permission of the World Health Organization (WHO) to estimate the ten-year fracture risk for each particular patient. The FRAX tool uses a number of factors, including bone density, to estimate your risk for breaking a hip or other major bone over the next ten years.

One of the main factors used in calculating FRAX is Bone Mineral Density, or BMD. Below is a sample Bone Density Report. Your report may not look exactly like this

)ut it should have the same basic key information.

BONE DENSITY REPORT

Name: Sex: Age:

Patient ID#:   Ethnicity: Height:

Referring Provider: DOB: Weight:

Bone Density   Exam Date: Exam Location:

Region:	BMD	T-Score	Z-Score	Classification
AP Spine (L1-L4)				
Femoral Neck(L)				
Total Hip (L)				
Femoral Neck(R)				
Total Hip (R)				

The Region denotes the area of your body which was scanned to test bone density. Your AP Spine L1-L4 are four of the five lumbar vertebrae between your rib cage and your pelvis. AP stands for anteroposterior, which means front to back. The head of your femur, or thigh bone, is a ball that sits inside your hip socket. The femoral neck sits just below the femoral head and is the most common location of a hip fracture.

The BMD column will list your Bone Mineral Density as found during the DEXA scan for each location.

A T-score is the comparison of your BMD to the BMD of a healthy thirty-year-old of the same sex. A T-score of -1.0 or above indicates normal bone density. A T-score between -1.0 and -2.5 indicates osteopenia, or low bone density. A T-score of -2.5 or below indicates osteoporosis. Multiplying your T-score by 10% yields a rough estimate of how much your bone density has decreased.

Why?

A Z-score is the comparison of your BMD to the average person of your same age and sex.

Your FRAX score should be listed on your DEXA scan report. If you do not see it there, ask your physician. Your personal FRAX score will estimate your risk for breaking a hip or other major bone over the next ten years.

Regarding Fracture Risk

Your bone density is only one factor used to compute your fracture risk. You must look at all your risk factors to help determine your ten-year fracture risk. That is why doctors developed the FRAX. The FRAX gives you a score which predicts your risk of fracturing a bone in the next ten years.

To assess your FRAX score, you fill out a questionnaire. The FRAX uses a formula which includes:

- Your age
- Your weight
- Your height

- Your gender
- Your smoking history/current smoking
- Your alcohol use (three or more drinks per day of any alcohol, including beer, wine, or liquor)
- Your fracture history
- Whether your parent fractured a hip
- Your glucocorticoid use
- Your history of rheumatoid arthritis
- Your bone mineral density

Once you complete the questionnaire, the program will compute your FRAX score, indicating the likelihood that you will suffer a major osteoporotic fracture in the next ten years and the likelihood you will fracture your hip in the next ten years. The program then plots your score on a graph. If your FRAX score is over five percent (5%) at age 70 or over, your doctor will recommend treatment and lifestyle changes. If you have a lower FRAX score but are younger, you will likely receive the same recommendation. Please see the next chapter to help you assess where and how you can make those lifestyle changes.

Chapter Four
Interventions to Increase Bone Density and Reduce Fracture Risk

M ost of these interventions are nothing new. Perhaps you will laugh when you read the list, or think you didn't need to read this book to come to this conclusion. You might say to yourself, "Tell me something I don't know."

You may be correct, or partially so. These are tried-and-true basics for health. That is precisely why I have included them here. I have tried them, personally, and found them to be effective.

These interventions include:

1. Walk.
2. Don't Fall.
3. Take Your Vitamins and Minerals.
4. Targeted Physical Therapy
5. Use a Vibroplate Machine.

Walk

I know what you're thinking. You're kidding, right?

I'm not kidding.

You have read my story of the ups and downs of my bone density. Of my year of panic. Of everything I did to strengthen my bones. What I discovered was that, if I walked almost every day, my NTX—you remember, the bone turnover marker—was much improved. If I stopped walking, even if I were jumping rope, doing banded exercise, which pulls strongly on the bones, even with all of that, my DEXA scan would show a decrease in my bone density.

So, walk. I'm not kidding.

But you have to get out there. Think every day. No matter the weather, unless it's so icy you think you may fall. (See #2, above and below). If you live in a cold climate, get crampons. Buy a treadmill and use it. But walk. Walk as much as you can. Walk an hour a day. At least thirty minutes. Make sure your heels register on the pavement or other walking surface so your bones get the benefit of the impact. During the year of covid-19, when confined to the house for months, I walked three to five miles almost every day. I walked over one hundred miles a month. In September of that year, Dr. Franzese did lab work on me and asked me what I had been doing differently. She advised that my NTX had dropped dramatically and was the lowest it had been since she had been treating me over a period of five and a half years. My body was not breaking down bone faster than I could build it. It's because I walked. After the blood work, I had stopped walking due to other constraints on my time. Even though I had purchased a year's subscription to the app of a fantastic fitness trainer, Kira Stokes, and I was using it religiously, at my DEXA scan four months later, my hip bones showed a decrease in density.

Since I was in the middle of writing this book, I freaked out. I thought I should stop writing the book because, clearly, I had failed at my own game. I felt like such an imposter. After some retrospection, however, I realized it was the perfect time for me to write it. I needed my own counsel, my own help, my own advice, to take a cold, hard look at what I had been doing for the past six to twelve months and to correct it. The reality was, I had become blasé and burned out taking so many supplements. I was concerned that I was taking too much calcium, and that it might have a negative effect on my cardiovascular system, on my arteries. I dove in, again, even though it was against my will. It felt like a chore. Why wouldn't this problem go away? It felt insurmountable.

But it was necessary. I was still in my late fifties and I did not want to ignore the state of my bones. I had to be a grown up and take a closer look. So, I did. I reviewed my own notes and the data from all the work I had done over the years. I rediscovered the value of walking. After getting my updated DEXA scan, I once again began walking a minimum of three miles per day. One month later, the benefit of walking for my bones showed up in my follow-up bloodwork: my bone turnover rate had once again decreased.

Don't Fall

Yes, this is also a tidbit of wisdom in the world of thinning bones. I was as surprised as you are to read this simple directive in a multitude of places, in books and online. The exhortation not to fall might seem simplistic and also out of your control. After all, who sets out to fall? It's not as if you have written it into your daily planner.

But there are some things you can control as a preventative measure to try and follow this command. Think about it. If you are like me, you go running around the house because you are in a hurry to get things done. Hurry, hurry, hurry. You run up and down the stairs. This mentality is even embedded in our language. I often use this verb. I will tell my husband, "I'm gonna run to the store." He'll respond, "Walk."

I'm the kind of person who used to look at the street signs that flash, "Don't walk" and say, "Don't Walk, Run!" And I would. Run, that is. But I have learned to slow down. I have learned not to walk quickly through the house in the dark. To turn on the light in the stairwell before I go up or down. To be cautious about leaving things on the floor that could turn into tripping hazards. To be cautious when going out in the snow and ice, knowing that a fall can mean a broken bone.

This does not mean you have to live in a bubble or give up the activities you have loved and enjoyed. Do you ski? Ride horses? You will have to take into consideration all of the risk factors, do your risk assessment (see Chapter Three), and make your own decisions about what and how you will live your life. The removal of activities that bring us joy can diminish our quality of life and make us feel old before our time. That isn't healthy. Consider reading one of the books listed at the end of this book in Appendix A: *The Myth of Osteoporosis. what every woman needs to know about creating bone health.*, by Gillian Sanson. She and her family members have a family history of osteopenia, even the younger ones. They have learned to live with it. You may want to read what she has to say.

Take Your Vitamins and Minerals

For some reason, medical doctors will tell patients with osteopenia and osteoporosis to take calcium and vitamin D, but they will not include the rest of the vitamins and minerals which are considered critical to the formation of new bone.

The fact that the human body requires these elements

secret. You can easily look up this information nd read it in a wide array of books. Yet, despite the number of doctors I visited in my quest for answers to my thinning bones, not one of them advised me about these crucial vitamins and minerals. Nevertheless, bones will not form properly without them. Worse still, if you take too much calcium without some of these vitamins and minerals, you could do permanent harm to your body, including to your cardiovascular system and to your kidneys.

Take this seriously, and look at Chapter Five where I set out the entire list for your review and use. This, and this alone, has changed bone strength and bone density for some people.

Targeted Physical Therapy

Physical therapy is an effective means of stimulating bone growth in people with low bone density. Such a regimen will contain both strengthening and resistance exercises. A licensed physical therapist can provide you with individualized exercise to strengthen your bones, and to improve your balance and posture. Good balance will help reduce the risk of falls and subsequent fractures. Proper posture will remove stress from your spine to reduce the likelihood of spinal fracture.

Vibration Plate Machine

What is a vibration plate machine? Good question. I

had never heard of one until Dr. Franzese told
the first time I had ever met her. After I left he
researched the heck out of it.

I discovered that whole body vibration was first ᴜ
effectively by the Soviet space program which enabled
their cosmonauts to remain in space for 420 days as
opposed to the American astronauts who returned home
after only 120 days. Despite an almost quadruple amount
of time in space, the cosmonauts did not suffer the severe
loss of strength and bone density that had plagued them in
the past. The only difference was the use of Whole Body
Vibration technology.

Essentially, a whole-body vibration plate machine,
also called a vibroplate machine or a vibration training
machine, is a compact piece of equipment that has a plate
which moves one of two ways: up and down or sideways
like a seesaw and vibrates at the rate of frequency of your
choice. When you stand, squat, or balance on your hands
or elbows on the plate, the plate causes your muscles to
contract and release involuntarily. For instance, the plate
of one brand of vibration plate vibrates at 25-50 times per
second, resulting in corresponding muscle activation. If
the user performs an exercise at 30Hz for 30 seconds, that
action will provoke a phenomenal 900 muscle actions. A
variety of studies suggest that the user can accelerate the
growth of bone, muscle, and balance at an exponentially
faster rate.

However, the use of a vibroplate machine to build

bone density is controversial. Some people claim that using a vibroplate machine for even fifteen minutes per day will help you lose weight, burn fat, build muscle, improve flexibility, and decrease your level of the stress hormone cortisol. Plenty of athletes and celebrities have used vibration training machines as part of their workouts, including Apolo Ohno, the late Kobe Bryant, Olympic cyclist Ruth Winder, the Denver Broncos, Mark Wahlberg, Cindy Crawford, Clint Eastwood, Joana Krupa, Courtney Cox, some Olympic athletes, the Raiders, the Steelers, the Dodgers, and the Bears. While I did not review all the literature for those claims, I did find good, solid evidence that the use of a vibroplate machine will likely build your bone density. Furthermore, Whole Body Vibration, or WBV, is proven to improve balance and therefore help to remove the risk of falling, which is a direct cause of fracture.

Research studies have yielded the following results:

- The high-frequency loading of the skeleton through 6-12 months of WBV leads to enhancements of bone mineral density in the hip.[19]

---

[19] Verschueren SMP, et al. "Effect of 6-month whole body vibration training on hip density, muscle strength, and postural control in postmenopausal women: a randomized controlled pilot study." *J Bone Miner Res.* 2004: 19:352-359. Accessed February 12, 2021; Gusi N, et al. "Low-frequency vibratory exercise reduces the risk of bone fracture more than walking: a randomized controlled trial." *BMC Musculoskelet Disord.* 2006;7:92.

- WBV training yielded significant improvement in total hip bone mineral density in a first-of-its-kind study of WBV involving elderly women, mean age 79.6.[20]

- In a 2006 study by Gusi et al, women who utilized WBV three times per week for eight months had a 4.3% increase in the BMD in the femoral neck of their hips. The results determined that the use of WBV is more effective than walking to improve women's bone mineral density and balance, both factors in fracture rate.[21]

- In a 2019 study, women engaging in 12 months of WBV significantly increased the BMD in their lumbar spine.[22]

- Women who trained using WBV for 24 weeks obtained significant increases of 5.15% in their

---

[20] Verscheuren SMP, et al. "The effects of whole-body vibration training and vitamin D supplementation on muscle strength, muscle mass, and bone density in institutionalized elderly women: A 6-month randomized, controlled trial." *J Bone Miner Res.* 2010;26(1):42-49. Doi.org/10.1002/jbmr.181. Accessed February 12, 2021.

[21] Gusi N, et al. "Low-frequency vibratory exercise reduces the risk of bone fracture more than walking: a randomized controlled trial." *BMC Musculoskelet Disord.* 2006;7:92. DOI: 10.1186/1471-2474-7-92. Accessed February 12, 2021.

[22] Jepsen, DB, et al. "The combined effect of Parathyroid hormone (1-34) and whole-body Vibration exercise in the treatment of postmenopausal Osteoporosis (PaVOS study): a randomized controlled trial." *Osteoporos Int* 2019;30(9):1827-1836. DOI:10.1007/s00198-019-05029-z. Accessed February 12, 2021.

lumbar bone mineral density and 10.58% in their lumbar spine mineral content.[23]

- Low magnitude mechanical signals from WBV are anabolic to bone if applied at a high frequency (15-90 Hz). Such mechanical signals can increase several characteristics of healthy bone. "Preliminary studies in children with disabling conditions and post-menopausal women indicate that such signals can be efficacious in reversing and/or preventing bone loss." The authors of the study believed that WBV represented "a unique, non-pharmacological prophylaxis for osteoporosis."[24]

- A 2002 study demonstrated that extremely low level, high frequency (>20 Hz) mechanical stimuli can stimulate bone formation and enhance bone quantity (BMD) and quality. All of the results were achieved at 45 Hz. However, these data indicate the strong influence of genetic variability, not only on trabecular bone structure but also on the plasticity of trabecular bone to both anabolic

[23] Marin-Cascales et al. "Effects of Two Different Neuromuscular Training Protocols on Regional Bone Mass in Postmenopausal Women: A Randomized Controlled Trial." *Front Physiol.* 2019;10:846. DOI 10.3389/fphys.2019.00846. Accessed February 12, 2021.

[24] Rubin C, et al. "Low-level mechanical signals and their potential as a non-pharmacological intervention for osteoporosis." *Age Ageing.* 2006;35 (Suppl 2):ii32-ii36. doi: 10.1093/ageing/afl082. Accessed February 15, 2021.

and catabolic mechanical stimuli.[25]

There are more studies out there which you can easily find and read on the internet.

There are two types of WBV platforms: low-intensity vibration platforms intended for osteoporosis therapy and high-intensity platforms intended for exercise. Of the low-intensity vibration plate machines, there are also two types: one in which the whole plate oscillates up and down, and one in which the plate utilizes "reciprocating vertical displacements on the left and right side of a fulcrum" like a seesaw.[26]

This is the vibration plate machine I purchased:

https://www.amazon.com/Confidence-Fitness-Vibration-Trainer-Platform/dp/B08N4BRMSL

It is reasonably priced and can be delivered to your door.

Each session should last about 15 minutes. For the hip, participants can do a squat, deep squat, wide-stance squat, toe stance, and one-legged squat. The women in the Gusi

---

[25] Judex et al. "Genetic predisposition to low bone mass is paralleled by an enhanced sensitivity to signals anabolic to the skeleton." *FASEB J* 16(10)(2002):1280-1282. https://doi.org/10.1096/fj.01-0913fje Accessed February 15, 2021.

[26] Gusi N, et al. "Low-frequency vibratory exercise reduces the risk of bone fracture more than walking: a randomized controlled trial." *BMC Musculoskelet Disord.* 2006;7:92. DOI: 10.1186/1471-2474-7-92. Accessed February 12, 2021.

study did three (3) sessions of WBV per week for eight (8) months. Each session included six (6) one-minute bouts of WBV at 12.6 Hz in frequency and 3 cm in amplitude with 60 degrees of knee flexion. The participants rested one minute between each bout. The rest is critical for the muscle and bone building. If you do not rest in between, the muscle and bone will fatigue and you will not get the results you are seeking.

After reviewing the studies, I do 60 seconds in a wide-legged squat for my hips, followed by a 60-second rest. I do that interval eight times in a session. I follow that with a 60-second interval of a wide-legged tall stance, finding a posture in which I can feel the vibration in my spine. I follow that with a 60-second rest and do eight intervals of those per session as well. I try to do this a minimum of four times per week. This is particularly important for the spine, as it is difficult to create the type of mechanical load on the spine that increases bone density.

Multicomponent Exercise Programs

Exercise programs which include portions of strength training, aerobics, high impact and/or weight-bearing training, and whole-body vibration can help prevent decline in bone mass and may help to increase bone mass with aging, especially among the postmenopausal population.[27]

Other Interventions

- Don't smoke cigarettes.
- Reduce alcohol intake to 1-2 drinks per day.
- Sit less than four hours per day.
- Do a minimum of thirty (30) minutes of weight-bearing exercise per day. A simple test to determine whether an exercise is weight-bearing is whether your feet are touching the floor. Walking, running, and weight-lifting are weight-bearing exercise; swimming is not.
- Do a twelve-minute daily yoga routine which is proven to benefit bone density. Find it here: https://www.ncbi.nlm.nih.gov/pmc/articles/PMC4851231/ and here: https://sciatica.org/.
- Eat more plants and less animal products.
- Reduce the amount of salt you consume.
- Reduce your stress to reduce the amount of cortisol in your bloodstream. See Chapter Seven.
- If possible, stop taking prescription drugs like tranquilizers, sedatives, Avandia, Actos, steroids, anticonvulsant, antacids, heartburn medications, aromatase inhibitors, and

---

[27] Benedetti, Maria Grazia, et al. "The Effectiveness of Physical Exercise on Bone Density in Osteoporotic Patients." *BioMed research international* vol. 2018 4840531. 23 Dec.2018, doi:10.1155/2018/4840531.

Tamoxifen.

- Increase your weight to a minimum of 127 pounds if that would not increase your risk of other health issues.

- Ensure appropriate vitamin and mineral intake. See Chapter Five.

- Ensure proper diet.

- Reduce inflammation in the body. Inflammation is the cause of seventy percent of human disease. Consider Time-Restricted Eating, popularly referred to as Intermittent Fasting, to reduce inflammation. The basic idea is to fast for 16 hours per day, eating only in an eight-hour window of your choice. Consult your physician to determine whether this is right for you.

CHAPTER FIVE
ASSESS DIET AND SUPPLEMENTS

The Bone's Building Blocks

The body requires essential minerals in order to build bone. The dairy industry has touted calcium as the main ingredient. Without the other vital minerals and vitamins, however, the body cannot construct bone or prevent its resorption.

The dairy controversy is worth its own chapter. The dairy industry has one of the greatest commercials of all time: Who doesn't know the question, Got milk? paired with a milk mustache and a food, like Oreo cookies, that pairs well? Milk is wholesome, right? Milk does a body good, right? Well, think again. It's not so clear-cut. It may be that the dairy industry just has a great lobby and has been a strong commercial force in this and other countries. Consider that the nations which consume the most dairy have the most osteoporosis. Consider that a diet high in animal products can leach calcium from your bones. Consider that Asian women, whose bones are tiny and who consume little to no calcium, have lower fracture rates than women who live in calcium-

ng nations.[28] Consider that calcium does not
e. To make strong bones, a body needs many
building blocks which are listed in the following
pages.

One thing to keep in mind as you are monitoring your body for appropriate levels of vitamins and minerals is that studies have demonstrated that, although blood tests may indicate sufficient levels, your tissues can still be deficient.[29]

Recent history is replete with examples. For instance, the National Basketball Association player Bill Walton had been sidelined several times in 1978 when his bones kept breaking and refused to heal.[30] Perplexed, his physician consulted with biologist Paul Saltman of the University of California, San Diego. Through testing, Dr. Saltman discovered Walton was deficient in three minerals which are critical to bone building: copper, zinc, and manganese. After treatment with these and other supplements, Walton's foot healed, the repeated fractures stopped, and he went back to

[28] Lanou, Amy Joy et al. *building bone vitality*. McGraw Hill 2009.
[29] Gaby, Alan R., M.D. *Preventing & Reversing Osteoporosis*. Three Rivers Press 1994 New York, New York. Pp 51. Accessed December 17, 2020.
[30] Gaby, Alan R., M.D. *Preventing & Reversing Osteoporosis*. Three Rivers Press 1994 New York, New York. Pp 29-31. Accessed December 17, 2020.

playing basketball. [31] Thereafter, x-rays of Walton's bones revealed they were denser than before the supplementation.[32]

Thereafter, postmenopausal women in a study were given manganese, magnesium, calcium, vitamin C, B vitamins, vitamin D, zinc, copper, boron, and other nutrients combined with other essential minerals and hormone replacement therapy for eight to nine months. They also avoided processed foods, limited their protein intake, consumed more vegetable than animal protein, and limited their consumption of salt, sugar, alcohol, coffee, tea, chocolate, and tobacco.[33] At the end of the study, the participants had increased their bone density by a "remarkable 11%, compared to only 0.7% in women" who had received hormone replacement therapy alone.[34]

These are just a few examples of the need for the consumption of essential vitamins and minerals which are critical to bone building and bone stabilization. In order to ensure your body has the right components to build your bones, you should ensure you are getting the

---

[31]PeaceHealth.org/medicaltopics/id/hn2881000# Accessed December 17, 2020.

[32] Gaby, Alan R., M.D. *Preventing & Reversing Osteoporosis*. Three Rivers Press 1994 New York, New York. Pp 29-31. Accessed December 17, 2020..

[33]PeaceHealth.org/medicaltopics/id/hn2881000# Accessed December 17, 2020.

[34] Ibid.

right amount of the following nutrients.

Vitamin K

Vitamin K is critical to bone formation. It is needed for the production of osteocalcin, "a protein found in large amounts of bone," and only in bone.[35] Vitamin K facilitates the migration of calcium to bone tissue, and facilitates the mineralization of bone.[36] It also reduces calcium excretion. The overuse of antibiotics likely destroys friendly intestinal bacteria which produce vitamin K. However, a high fiber diet, along with garlic, dark green leafy vegetables, and acidophilus, can help restore appropriate levels. Dr. Alan R. Gaby, a well-renowned physician who focuses on healing the body with nutrition, recommends 150-500 mcg per day.[37] Do not take large amounts of vitamin K due to its toxicity at high levels, and do not take it at all if you are prescribed coumadin or warfarin.[38]

Manganese

Manganese stimulates the production of mucopolysaccharides, which are protein-like molecules that provide a structure in bones for calcification to take

[35] Gaby, Alan R., M.D. *Preventing & Reversing Osteoporosis*. Three Rivers Press 1994 New York, New York. Pp 22. Accessed December 17, 2020.
[36] Ibid.
[37] Ibid at p 27.
[38] Ibid.

place. Environmental pollution, food processing, and farming techniques lower the amount of manganese we ingest. In order to get enough manganese, eat whole grains, nuts, seeds, leafy vegetables, meat, and rice polish (also known as rice bran). To prevent diminishing the amount of manganese in your body, avoid the food additive EDTA, and avoid sugar, white rice, and white flour. Dr. Gaby recommends taking 15-20 mg of manganese per day. Make sure not to take an excessive amount as it may cause toxicity.[39]

Magnesium

Up to fifty percent of all magnesium in the body is found in the skeleton. If you are deficient in magnesium, it is likely you have or will develop osteoporosis or abnormal calcification of bone. To ensure appropriate magnesium levels in the body, eat whole grains, nuts, seeds, green vegetables, and animal foods. Take 250-600 mg per day unless you have renal failure, then seek out the advice of your physician.[40] To avoid depleting the magnesium levels present in your body, avoid processed foods, too much alcohol, and too much stress (adrenaline causes magnesium to be flushed out of the cells). Limit consumption of refined sugar, salt, alcohol, coffee, tea, chocolate, and tobacco. Limit protein intake,

---

[39] Ibid at pp 31-36.
[40] Ibid at pp 41-42.

and prefer vegetable protein over animal protein.[41]

Reduce Animal Protein

Americans consume more cow's milk and products per person than most populations in the world. However, American women aged 50 or over have one of the highest rates of hip fractures in the world.[42]

An impressively strong association exists between animal protein consumption and bone fracture rate for women in different countries.[43] This study was written by researchers at Yale University School of Medicine and summarized data on protein intake and fracture rates taken from thirty-four (34) separate surveys in sixteen (16) countries that were published in twenty-nine (29) peer-reviewed research publications. All of the subjects were women aged fifty (50) or older. The conclusion was that seventy percent (70%) of the fracture rate was attributable to the consumption of animal protein.[44]

---

[41] Gaby, Alan R., M.D. *Preventing & Reversing Osteoporosis.* Three Rivers Press 1994 New York, New York. Pp 41-42. Accessed December 17, 2020.

[42] Frasetto LA, todd KM, Morris C, Jr., et al. "Worldwide incidence of hip fracture in elderly women: relation to consumption of animal and vegetable foods." *J. Gerontology* 55 (2000): M585-M592.

[43] Abelow, BJ, Holford TR, and Insogna KL. "Cross-cultural association between dietary animal protein and hip fracture: a hypothesis." *Calcif. Tissue Int.* 50 (1992): 14-18.

[44] Ibid.

Animal protein increases the acid load in the body.[45] In order to neutralize the acid, the body uses calcium from the bones, thus weakening them and creating a greater fracture risk . This increases the amount of calcium in the urine. [46] This is well-studied, well-documented, and demonstrates that the amount of animal protein eaten by typical Americans is capable of causing substantial increases in urinary calcium.[47]

Doubling protein intake (mostly animal protein) from 35-78 g/day causes an alarming 50% increase in urinary calcium.[48]

A study from the Department of Medicine at the University of California, San Francisco published in 2000, used eighty-seven (87) surveys from thirty-three (33) countries and compared the ratio of vegetable to animal protein consumption to the rate of bone fractures.[49] A high ratio of vegetable to animal protein consumption was found to be strongly associated with a

---

[45] Wachsman, A and Berstein DS. "Diet and osteoporosis." *Lancet* May 4, 1968 (1968): 958-959
[46] Campbell, T. Colin, and Campbell, TM. The China Study. (2006): 204-211
[47] Campbell, T. Colin, and Campbell, TM. The China Study. (2006): 204-211
[48] Ibid.
[49] Frasetto LA, todd KM, Morris C, Jr., et al. "Worldwide incidence of hip fracture in elderly women: relation to consumption of animal and vegetable foods." *J. Gerontology* 55 (2000): M585-M592.

virtual disappearance of bone fractures.[50]

These studies are compelling because they were published in leading research journals, the authors were careful in their analyses and interpretation of data, they included a large number of individual research reports, and the statistical significance of the association of animal protein with bone fracture rates is truly exceptional.

The Study of Osteoporotic Fractures Research Group at the University of California at San Francisco published yet another study of over 1,000 women aged sixty-five and up. Like the multi-country study, researchers characterized women's diets by the proportions of animal and plant protein. After seven years of observations, the women with the highest ratio of animal protein to plant protein had 3.7 times more bone fractures than the women with the lowest ratio. Also, during this time, the women with the high ratio lost bone almost four times as fast as the women with the lowest ratio.[51]

In the China study, where the animal-to-plant ratio was about ten percent (10%), the fracture rate is only one-fifth that of the U.S. Nigeria shows an animal-to-

---

[50] Campbell, T. Colin, and Campbell, TM. The China Study. (2006): 204-211
[51] Sellmeyer, DE, Stone KL, Sebastian A, et al. "A high ratio of dietary animal to vegetable protein increases the rate of bone loss and the risk of fracture in postmenopausal women." *Am. J. Clin. Nutr.* 73 (2001): 118-122

plant protein ratio of only about ten percent (10%) that of Germany, and the hip fracture incidence is lower by ninety-nine percent (99%).[52]

Therefore, the "calcium bonanza" is not justified.[53] In another study of ten countries, a high intake of calcium was associated with a higher—not lower—risk of bone fracture.[54] Researchers believe that excessively high intakes of calcium consumed over a long time impair the body's ability to control how much calcium it uses and when.[55] If too much calcium is used over a long period of time, the body may lose its ability to regulate calcitriol, permanently or temporarily disrupting the regulation of calcium absorption and excretion.[56] Ruining the regulatory mechanism in this way is a recipe for osteoporosis in menopausal and post-menopausal women. The fact that the body loses its ability to control finely tuned mechanisms when they are subjected to continuous abuse is a well-established

[52] Frasetto LA, todd KM, Morris C, Jr., et al. "Worldwide incidence of hip fracture in elderly women: relation to consumption of animal and vegetable foods." *J. Gerontology* 55 (2000): M585-M592; Campbell, T. Colin, and Campbell, TM. The China Study. (2006): 204-211

[53] Campbell, T. Colin, and Campbell, TM. The China Study. (2006): 204-211

[54] Ibid.

[55] Campbell, T. Colin, and Campbell, TM. The China Study. (2006): 204-211

[56]Campbell, T. Colin, and Campbell, TM. The China Study. (2006): 204-211

phenomenon in biology.[57]

Bone mineral density is not the deciding factor. There are geographical areas in which overall bone mass and bone mineral content measurements are lower than they are in "Western" countries, but the fracture rate is also lower, defying accepted logic of how we define "big, strong bones."[58], [59], [60], [61].

Seventy-one percent of the studies reviewed by Dr. Amy Joy Lanou in *building bone vitality* showed that soy foods improve BMD, decrease urinary calcium excretion, or reduce fracture risk.[62] Lanou, an assistant professor of health and wellness at the University of North Carolina, found compelling evidence that soy foods strengthen bone, including:

- Vanderbilt University researchers tracked soy consumption and fractures among 24,403 postmenopausal Chinese women for 4.5 years.

---

[57] Ibid.

[58] Ibid.

[59] Ho, SC. "Body measurements, bone mass, and fractures: does the East differ from the West?" *Clin. Orthopaed. Related Res.* 323 (1996): 75-80.

[60] Aspray, JF, Prentide A, Cole TJ, et al. "Low bone mineral content is common but osteoporotic fractures are rare in elderly rural Gambian women." J. Bone Min. Res. 11 (1996): 1019-1025

[61] Tsai, K-S. "Osteoporotic fracture rate, bone mineral density, and bone metabolism in Taiwan." J. Formosan Med. Assoc. 96 (1997): 802-805.

[62] Lanou, Amy Joy et al. *building bone vitality*. McGraw Hill 2009, p 124.

As soy intake increased, fracture risk decreased. Compared with those who ate the least soy, women who consumed the most suffered twenty-four percent (24 %) fewer fractures.[63]

- Yale researchers fed women identical diets, except for the source of the protein—meat for a while, then soy. While eating the meat, their urine became considerably more acidic.[64]

- Iowa State University researchers fed sixty-nine (69) menopausal women a placebo (3 oz per day) or soy protein. After six months, bone loss occurred in the placebo group, but in the soy group, BMD increased.[65]

- Japanese researchers measured the urinary calcium of women provided the same diet plus either meat or soy. In the meat group, urinary calcium excretion increased markedly. But in the soy group, it did not change.[66]

- Hong Kong researchers surveyed the soy intake of four hundred fifty-four (454) postmenopausal Chinese women and then measured their bone mineral density. As soy food consumption increased, so did their BMD.[67]

---

[63] Ibid at 125.
[64] Ibid.
[65] Ibid.
[66] Lanou, Amy Joy et al. *building bone vitality*. McGraw Hill 2009, p 125.
[67] Ibid.

- Chinese researchers gave ninety (90) women one of three dietary supplements: a placebo, or low or high amounts of soy. After six months, BMD declined in the placebo group but increased in both soy groups, with the greatest increase among those who consumed the high-soy supplement.[68]

Folic Acid

Folic acid significantly reduces homocysteine levels. Homocysteine results when methionine breaks down in the body. It appears to be a harmful substance and can build up in the body after menopause, causing osteoporosis. The amount of folic acid you need may depend upon the amount of animal protein you consume. Animal protein contains methionine, which causes the level of homocysteine in your body to rise. Dr. Gaby implies that five mg per day is likely to be sufficient; however, it is impossible to get five mg per day from diet alone. Eat fresh vegetables, wheat germ, and Brewer's yeast to obtain folic acid naturally, and supplement it with five mg per day. Be careful, however, as folic acid may interfere with diagnostic tests for anemia; it can interact with common drugs and nutrients, Dilantin in particular, and may therefore cause the return of seizures in those individuals taking

---

[68] Ibid.

Dilantin to prevent seizures.[69] Talk with your doctor if you find yourself in this situation.

Boron

Boron supplements appear to reduce calcium excretion from the body by forty-four (44%). They also increase the amount of 17β-estradiol and testosterone in the body, equivalent to the amount in women who were receiving estrogen replacement therapy, further suggesting its key role in the prevention of bone loss. Scientist also believe that boron increases the blood level of vitamin D. Dr. Gaby suggests taking 1-3 mg per day in addition to getting it naturally in daily consumption of fruits and vegetables.[70]

Vitamin B-6

Like folic acid, vitamin B-6 reduces homocysteine levels in the blood. Moreover, it also provides "tensile strength and structure to collagen and other structural proteins in bone tissue," writes Dr. Gaby in *Preventing & Reversing Osteoporosis*. Vitamin B-6 "may also influence the production of the bone-building hormone, progesterone." Environmental pollution appears to increase human need for vitamin B-6. Get vitamin B-6 in whole grains, watermelon, bananas, fish, chicken, beef, tomatoes, and some nuts. Dr. Gaby recommends supplementing this with 25-50 mg per day. Be aware

---

[69] Ibid at pp 51-55.
[70] Ibid at pp 58-59.

that, if you consume a high-protein diet or smoke, you will need more. If you have asthma, carpal tunnel syndrome, premenstrual syndrome, you may need 50-200 mg per day. However, do not take more than 100 mg per day without talking with your doctor.[71]

Zinc

Zinc enhances biochemical actions of vitamin D, is foundational for the formation of osteoblasts (bone-building cells) and osteoclasts (cells which facilitate bone resorption), and for the synthesis of protein found in bone tissue. Zinc deficiency is common. Boost your levels of zinc by consuming whole grains, meat, chicken, poultry, and legumes, and by taking 15-30 mg per day along with 2 mg of copper.[72] Take zinc picolinate, zinc citrate, or chelated zinc, but not zinc sulfate.[73]

Strontium

In his 1994 treatise, *Preventing & Reversing Osteoporosis*, Dr. Gaby recommends strontium supplementation. Many people have a negative reaction when they hear about strontium. That association comes

---

[71] Ibid at pp 71-77.
[72] Zinc interferes with the body's use of copper, and the American diet is typically low in copper.
[73] Gaby, Alan R., M.D. *Preventing & Reversing Osteoporosis*. Three Rivers Press 1994 New York, New York. Pp 82-83. Accessed December 17, 2020.

from strontium-90, the radioactive substance produced by nuclear fission. Strontium itself is a naturally-occurring chemical element which is necessary for bone health. Early studies of strontium yielded very encouraging data about its ability to facilitate remineralization of bone. In one study, participants who took 600-700 mcg per day for six months increased their bone formation by a whopping 172%. For a period of time, strontium was available in the European Union under the brand name Protelos/Osseor for the treatment of osteoporosis. Unfortunately, it was discovered that strontium can interfere with accurate DEXA scan readings as it replaces calcium in the bones. This will yield inaccurate readings of bone density increase, since strontium does not make new bone. In addition, subsequent data showed significant increases in both heart attack and blood clots in patients taking strontium ranelate. Other harmful effects were associated with strontium ranelate, including skin reactions, seizures, liver inflammation, disturbances in thinking, and reduced amount of red blood cells. For these reasons, the European Medicines Agency's Pharmacovigilance Risk Assessment Committee recommended that strontium no longer be used to treat osteoporosis.[74] As a result, Protelos/Osseor and another strontium product, Servier, were removed from the market. A generic form

[74] *Why Strontium Is Not Advised for Bone Health*. American Bone Health. www.americanbonehealth.org. Accessed February 26, 2021.

of strontium is still available for use in the European Union from Aristo Pharma Ltd., for those who have no other treatment, but only with special precautions and strong warnings. Strontium in a different form (strontium citrate, for example) is available in the United States as a dietary supplement. For all these reasons, while Dr. Gaby recommended it in 1994, its use appears ill-advised unless you have no other viable alternative. In particular, it is contraindicated for those with blood clots or history of blood clots, for people who have limited mobility, for patients with a history of cardiac issues, and for those with high blood pressure not under good control.[75] If you decide to take it after discussion with your physician, you can take strontium carbonate or strontium gluconate, which is easier to absorb and likely the reason that the second study I cite, above, administered lesser amounts of strontium to participants.

Copper

Copper is another key micronutrient in the formation of bone tissue. It is found in whole grains, nuts, organ meats, eggs, poultry, legumes, and green leafy vegetables. A dose of 1-2 mg per day should be sufficient unless you take large amounts of zinc. If that is the case, you should increase your dose to 3-4 mg per

---

[75] *Strontium for Osteoporosis*. www.webmd.com. Accessed February 26, 2021.

day.[76]

Silicon

Silicon helps to form cartilage and other connective tissue.[77] Scientists have demonstrated that a silicon-deficient diet causes gross abnormalities of the skull and temporal bones. You can consume it naturally in rice polish, rice bran, and brown rice; horsetail; unrefined whole grains such as barley, oats, wheat bran; beer; green beans, spinach, root vegetables, and seafood. Supplementing the diet is advisable. BioSil is the most bioavailable supplement, and dosage is recommended on the packaging. BioSil is available on Amazon.

Vitamin C

This versatile vitamin promotes "formation and crosslinking of some of the structural proteins found in bone."[78] Supplementation with 500 mg per day is encouraged, but not more than 1,000 mg per day in the

---

[76] Gaby, Alan R., M.D. *Preventing & Reversing Osteoporosis.* Three Rivers Press 1994 New York, New York. P 94. Accessed January 11, 2021. Dr. Gaby actually recommended an increase to "several" mg per day. An online search helped me translate "several" to "3-4."
[77] Gaby, Alan R., M.D. *Preventing & Reversing Osteoporosis.* Three Rivers Press 1994 New York, New York. P 95. Accessed January 11, 2021.
[78] Gaby, Alan R., M.D. *Preventing & Reversing Osteoporosis.* Three Rivers Press 1994 New York, New York. P 96. Accessed January 11, 2021.

presence of chronic renal failure or coumadin.[79]

Vitamin D

Vitamin D is necessary for the absorption of calcium and its deposit into bone tissue. It also plays a critical role in muscle strength. The human body makes vitamin D when the skin is exposed to the sun. Otherwise, we consume it in fortified dairy products, fish, eggs, and liver. Supplementation of 200-400 units per day is recommended.[80] However, at least one study indicated that, in elderly women, mean age of 79.6 years, 400 IU is not sufficient to prevent fracture. That study recommended the use of 700-800 IU of vitamin D to reduce fracture risk in elderly women.[81] Supplementation with 1, 25-dihydroxyvitamin D3 can cause dangerous elevations in serum calcium, so it is wise to confer with your doctor about the type and amount you are taking.[82]

---

[79] Ibid at 97.

[80] Ibid at 98.

[81] Bischoff-Ferrari HA, et al. "Estimation of optimal serum concentrations of 25-hyroxyvitamin D for multiple health outcomes." *Am J Clin Nutr.* 2006;84:18-28. Accesssed February 12, 2021; Verscheuren SMP, et al. "The effects of whole-body vibration training and vitamin D supplementation on muscle strength, muscle mass, and bone density in institutionalized elderly women: A 6-month randomized, controlled trial." *J Bone Miner Res.* 2010;26:1:42-49. Doi.org/10.1002/jbmr.181. Accessed February 12, 2021 .

[82] Ibid.

Calcium

Calcium is one of the many important nutrients in preventing and treating osteoporosis, but it cannot stand on its own, or when paired only with vitamin D. Dr. Gaby cites concerns with taking too much calcium, especially if you do not take enough magnesium. Too much calcium can cause dangerous conditions, including calcium plaque buildup, and can interfere with the absorption of iron. Too much calcium paired with too little magnesium can cause osteoporosis and soft-tissue calcification. There is also a close correlation between osteoporosis and calcification of the abdominal aorta.[83] Some practitioners recommend a 2:1 ratio of calcium to magnesium; others recommend just the opposite, a 1:2 ratio of calcium to magnesium. Dr. Gaby recommends using a smaller dose of all the required nutrients for the best outcome.[84]

Selenium

Selenium is an essential trace element which appears to be necessary for bone health in terms of reducing inflammation and oxidative stress. [85] The suggested dose is 55 mcg per day.

---

[83] Ibid at 108-109.
[84] Ibid at 105.
[85]Zeng, Huawei, et al. "Selenium in Bone Health: Roles in Antioxidant Protection and Cell Proliferation." *Nutrients* vol 5(1) Jan 2013 pp 97-110. doi:10.3390/nu5010097. Accessed January 11, 2021.

/ you will find a concise chart of these vitamins
:rals and the suggested daily requirements.

Supplement	Recommended Daily Requirement
Calcium Citrate	800 mg
Vitamin K2 (MK4)	150 - 500 mcg, divided, with calcium and D (Do not take excess.)*
Boron	3 mg
Strontium	500 - 2000 mg (s gluconate)**
Magnesium	Amino acid chelate. 250 - 600 mg
Omega -3 Fatty Acids	2000 mg EPA and DHA for heart health
Manganese	15 - 20 mg (Do not take excess.)*
Folic Acid	5 mg
B-6	25 - 50 mg (No more than 100 mg)*
Zinc	15 - 30 mg (z prolineate, z citrate, z chelated) Not sulfate
Copper	2 mg
Silicon	Biosil
Vitamin C	500 mg
Vitamin D	200 - 400 units
Selenium	55 mcg
Iron Fluoride	200 mcg

* More is not better.
** Use is controversial and may interfere with DEXA scan results.

For a downloadable one-sheet of this graphic, please
visit my website at www.jaynewesler.com.

I encourage you to read Dr. Alan Gaby's book
yourself so you can fully understand the critical role
these nutrients play. Please see Appendix A.

CHAPTER SIX
FIND A KNOWLEDGEABLE
PHYSICIAN

If you have a physician whom you know and trust, you should start with that professional. If you do not have a physician in whom you have faith and confidence, find one. Do an internet search. Ask around. Find a DO or an MD. A holistic practitioner may be more inclined to monitor you closely and work with you on interventions that do not include medication.

Once you have identified the appropriate professional, arrange to have a 30-minute visit. Set a clear agenda in advance. Advise the office staff that you would like to come in to discuss an IBP (Individual Bone-Building Plan) with the doctor.

Prior to your visit, create an agenda. Use your IBP. Be concise with your goals. Know what you want your doctor to do for you. For instance, do you want your doctor to discuss:

- all potential supplements with you
- your exercise routine, including physical therapy
- the use of appropriate blood work to monitor your NTX and bone density at appropriate intervals (see Monitoring, below).

Bring two copies of your agenda and IBP with you to the doctor visit. Share them with your doctor. Tell your doctor that you would like to take an assertive, proactive approach to building your bone density. Tell your doctor you would like them to partner with you. Review your goals and the tasks you would like your doctor to perform.

Monitoring

Have your doctor do appropriate testing to get a baseline and to find out how your body is functioning vis a vis your bones. Ask your doctor to order the following tests for you every four to six months.

Tests to Assess Bone Health

1. NTX 24-hour urine collection + second morning urine to measure bone turnover (N-Telopeptide)
2. Calcium levels
3. Parathyroid hormone
4. Thyroid Studies (TSH [thyroid stimulating hormone] T4, T3, reverse T3, thyroid auto-antibodies)
5. Basic chemistry panel/ CBC (Complete Blood

Count)

6. Celiac and anti-gliadin (gluten subunit) antibodies
7. Cortisol Serum
8. DHEA/DHEA-S
9. Sex Hormones
10. Vitamin and Mineral Studies (B12, folate, vitamin D, cellular magnesium, and zinc)
11. Urinalysis and Urine Microalbumin (pH)
12. Epstein Barr Virus (EBV) Antibodies
13. Urine Heavy Metals

Once you have gotten the blood work, you can develop and implement your bone-building plan of targeted interventions. See Chapter Eight for details. You and your doctor can then compare your progress at each visit so you can see what is working.

CHAPTER SEVEN
A WORD ABOUT STRESS

Much has been written about the effects of stress on the body. Stress activates our fight or flight response and releases cortisol into our system. In response, our body releases calcium, gleaned from our teeth and our bones, to help neutralize the effect of the cortisol and to restore the pH balance in the body.

If stress becomes chronic, our body will deplete the calcium stores in our bones faster than they can be replaced. The result could be bones that become more and more porous, more and more brittle, leading to a diagnosis of osteopenia or, worse, osteoporosis.

Stress impacts our lifestyle, and it's up to us to put a stop to it. Think **HALT**:

Hungry

Angry

Lonely

Tired

Keep an eye on yourself. If you are experiencing one or more of these states, do what the acronym tells you: HALT! These are the bigger red flags that signal you need something. Are you skipping meals or eating junk food? You may have a low blood sugar or just feel as if you are dragging. Are you frustrated with your work or yourself or angry with your kids or your partner? Face it head on and deal with it in an effective way. Are you feeling sad and lonely? Go out for a walk. Call a friend or family member. Join a Zoom or other group in your area through Meetup.com. Meetup is an event site where you can find a group that interests you and join. Are you tired? Can you take a rest, even a five-minute break? Shut your door and sit quietly in a chair. Don't look at your electronics. That will not be restful. Just breathe. In and out. In and out. Don't just do something. Sit there. Yes, you read that correctly. Don't just do something. Sit there. For five minutes. Practice sleep hygiene at home. Set an intended bed time and start getting ready at least an hour early. Do you have to get clothing and lunches ready for tomorrow? Schedule enough time to do that and to allow yourself some quiet time so you do not jump into bed as if you are sliding into home base and expect to fall asleep anytime soon.

We can add worries and fears to the list of stressors. Anxiety is the number one mental health issue in the world. It's easy to worry about important challenges and potential threats in our lives, and we do have to face those fears and make plans to take care of our responsibilities. However, once we do that, succumbing to fear and worry will just make us sick and give us more to worry about. It becomes a vicious cycle.

To address the stress, give yourself some effective tools and strategies:

Meditation. There are many ways to meditate, and there is no one right way. Stop and do it right now. Just stop. Close your eyes. Take a deep breath, then let it out slowly. Take another one, and make sure it goes into your belly. Many of us tend to breathe in a shallow way in which the breath goes in and out of our chest, but our bellies do not move. To calm yourself, you should imagine your breath going down into the belly, and let your belly expand, then contract with the slow exhalation of the breath. Just sit like that for five minutes, thinking of the breath. Follow it in, then out of the body. Breathe slowly. When a thought enters your awareness, allow it to drift right back out again, like a cloud. Once you are comfortable with this practice, consider extending the time to ten minutes. You can visit my website at www.jaynewesler.com to learn the many amazing benefits of meditation. You can also google Sa Ta Na Ma Meditation. This is an excellent meditation practice that helps improve memory and focus, reduces stress, and is a powerful, proven tool against Alzheimer's disease.

Tapping. Tapping, also known as Emotional Freedom Technique, or EFT, is an effective stress-reduction technique which uses acupressure principles to calm the fight or flight response, to regulate the nervous system, and to reduce anxiety. You can find an instructional video on my website at www.jaynewesler.com. Alternatively, www.thetappingsolution.com is an EFT website with excellent resources.

Yoga. Yoga is a mind-body practice that utilizes physical poses, breathing techniques, and meditation to increase health by lowering blood pressure, lowering heart rate, and reducing stress. Find a class online through YouTube. Try Lesley Fightmaster or your local studio, which may offer Zoom or other virtual classes.

Emotional Support. Sometimes it's important just to be heard. Do not negate the significance of human contact, empathy, and kindness. Reach out to someone and say you need a shoulder to lean on. You will make someone else's day because—guess what? —it's nice to be needed.

Get outside and soak in some sunshine. Spending time outdoors is important for our mental and physical health. Fresh air and sunshine are important. Sunshine reacts with our skin to produce vitamin D, a vitamin necessary for so many of the body's processes. Studies demonstrate the importance of Shinrin-Yoku, or forest bathing, for health and well-being

CHAPTER EIGHT
DEVELOP AN INDIVIDUAL BONE-BUILDING PLAN

The first thing you must do to create an IBP is to find your starting point. That is where your bones are at today. What does your DEXA scan show? Be brave. Get it out and take another look at it. It should include the numbers which identify how much bone gain or loss you have had and should also include your FRAX score. Whatever it is, you can face it.

Now you know your bone density. You know your FRAX score. You're a grown up, so you can face this thing. When you stop, take a breath, and think about the likelihood that you will sustain a fracture in the next ten years, it isn't as bad as you thought it was, right? You can feel positive and empowered to increase your bone density without medication.[86] The best way to do that is to make your own bone-building plan. Use the sample below to develop yours:

---

[86] If you would like to book a session to talk about this or for help creating an IBP, email me at jayne@jaynewesler.com.

INDIVIDUAL BONE-BUILDING PLAN

Name: Jane Doe

DEXA Scans:	March 2020	November 2020
LH		
LFN		
TH		
S		

Key: LH: Left Hip, LFN: Left Femoral Neck, TH: Total Hip, S: Spine

RISK FACTORS	INTERVENTION
• Female	
• Caucasian	
• Sit 4+ hours/day	Order a stand-and-walk desk. Stand more at work. Walk at lunch.
• Smoke	Stop! Get on Nicorette and go to smoking cessation groups. Consider hypnosis/hypnotherapy.
• 6-7 Alcoholic drinks/week	Consider reducing amount of consumption.
• Drink 5 cups coffee/day	Gradually reduce consumption. Replace with black or green tea or coffee substitute. Kaffree Roma.
• No exercise	Walk minimum 30 minutes per day total. Go to physical therapy and do the exercises three times per week. Add the twelve yoga poses daily (see Chapter Four). Add Whole Body Vibration.
	Sleep 7-8 hours per night.
	Ensure proper diet and supplements (see Chapter Five).
	No cola. Reduce tripping hazards.

For a downloadable one-sheet of this graphic, please visit my website at www.jaynewesler.com.

Make sure to insert the gain or loss into each column and row as indicated. For each DEXA scan you have, make another column and insert the numbers. This will give you a fast, easy way to track your progress over time. As you will see in the graphic, Jane Doe had two scans thus far, in March 2018 and November 2020.

Then ask yourself, What are my risk factors? Make a list of them in the left-hand column.

Now, for each risk factor that is subject to change, list in the right-hand column a lifestyle change that you can make or an intervention you can perform to neutralize or reduce the risk factor. For instance, if you drink five cups of coffee per day, work on gradually reducing that number from five to three, then from three to one. Consider switching to tea or to a coffee-substitute. Kaffree Roma is a pretty good substitute in that it tastes like coffee; even my coffee connoisseur mother admitted it tasted good.

Even though some of your risk factors are immutable, i.e., unable to be changed, you can still list other interventions you can take to increase your bone density. See Chapter Four for options.

Keep in mind that this is not a fast and fierce battle. You will need to maintain and stick to your plan, revising it as necessary over the months and years. Think of it as a lifestyle and incorporate the changes as you are able in order to fit them into your daily life. Consider including a level of accountability to yourself, to your family, and possibly to a professional such as your knowledgeable physician from Chapter Six.

Once you have made your IBP, hang it up on your refrigerator, bathroom mirror, or some other place where you will see it every day. Place encouraging post-it notes all over the house with your goals (Walk 30 minutes today!) and encouraging affirmations (I am powerful! I can increase my bone density!) all over your home, car, and workstation . Write them in lipstick on your bathroom mirror.

Make sure your IBP includes all aspects of bone building: nutrition, supplements, weight-bearing exercise, stress reduction, improving balance, fall reduction, and reduction of all risk factors.

Remember ODAAT. That's One Day At A Time. That's all you have to do.

Remember, too, that a decrease in bone density is not disease. It is part of the normal aging process. Do not harangue yourself if you have a bad day, miss your walk, have a cup of coffee. One day, one miss here and there, is not the issue. This is a lifestyle and a cumulative effect for which you are reaching over time. Be gentle with and good to yourself. Your body and your mind need that. Try to think of this as a new adventure and a new way of living. You will get used to it and will likely enjoy the changes to your life and your routine, and they will likely make you feel better and feel healthier.

Finally, there is nothing wrong with the decision to take medication to increase your bone density. We may all need to do that at some point. But before you agree to do that, you should know you have these other options.

CHAPTER NINE
YOU CAN DO IT!

As a result of my own diagnosis of osteoporosis, my struggle to find ways to build my own bone density, my success in doing so, and my continued struggles, there is a lot I have learned. I am well aware that we all have a finite period on the face of this earth. In keeping with many people-centric teachings of love, my fondest wish is to do good in this world. Like any other human, I was born with a number of talents: a gift for language, for the written word, empathy, compassion, and strong ambition. That is why I committed to write No Bones About It as a source of guidance, comfort, challenge, and practical interventions.

If you change only one thing, and you start walking regularly, you will give your bones a boost. If you commit to changing a few of your risk factors, you will change the health of your bones. If you will commit to create an Individual Bone Plan (IBP) for yourself and to follow it, you will likely increase your bone density to a point beyond which you would have believed possible.

Dear Reader, you have one life to live. You want to be strong and well to accomplish your dreams, to find joy and success and love in the world. There is still time for you. Make a promise to yourself now that you will do this for yourself, maybe even for your daughter or your niece so they, too, can learn and understand that our bodies can and will heal themselves. We just need to get out of the body's way and give it the things it needs. Keep reading to find out how. I did it, and you can, too.

Visit my website, JayneWesler.com to join my Facebook group, No Bones About It, to share your answers, tell your stories, and to find strength and validation.

Visit my website at JayneWesler.com to read my blogs on building bone density.

You will also see blogs about IBS, osteoporosis, and emotional tears.

Visit the Resources section on my website at

JayneWesler.com.

Please leave a 5-Star Review for No Bones About It: Increase Your Bone Density Without Medication at the retailer's webpage where you purchased this book!

APPENDIX A

I strongly recommend that you read the following in order to make sound decisions about your own battle for the bones:

Gaby, Alan R., M.D. Preventing & Reversing Osteoporosis. What You Can Do About Bone Loss. A Leading Expert's Natural Approach to Increasing Bone Mass. Three Rivers Press. New York. 1994.

Lanou, Amy Joy, Ph.D. and Castleman, Michael. building bone vitality. A Revolutionary Diet Plan to Prevent Bone Loss and Reverse Osteoporosis. McGraw Hill. 2009.

Sanson, Gillian. The Myth of Osteoporosis. what every woman needs to know about creating bone health. MCD Century Publications, LLC. 2011.

Schneider, Diane L. MD. *The Complete Book of Bone Health.* Prometheus Books. 2011.

Get the FREE Resources
That Come with This Book.

Make Sure You Access Them Here:
JayneWesler.com

Do you know anyone who has a child with special needs?

Do them a favor and refer them to Jayne Wesler's

Handbook for Parents of Children with Special Needs: A Therapeutic and Legal Approach.

Access it on:

JayneWesler.com

Also available on Amazon.

Know anyone who needs a good cry?
Know anyone who has been made to feel weak or
emotionally unstable by insensitive people simply
because they wear their heart on their sleeve?
This book is for you:

HURTS SO GOOD
AN ORGASM OF TEARS

Access it on:

JayneWesler.com

Also available on Amazon.

Know anyone who needs to deepen and strengthen their relationships?

Refer them to Jayne Wesler's

HURTS SO GOOD: AN ORGASM OF TEARS WORKBOOK

Learn how to deepen your most important relationships with exercises for emotional intimacy. You will be surprised how much your trust and your love for yourself and your partner will deepen when you utilize the activities and exercises in this extraordinary book.

Access it on:

JayneWesler.com

Also available on Amazon.

Made in the USA
Las Vegas, NV
22 January 2022

42078175R00083